Nita City Housing Authority

V.

Johnson

Second Edition

Nita City Housing Authority

V.

Johnson

Second Edition

Mark S. Caldwell

Public Program Development & Resource Director
National Institute for Trial Advocacy

NATIONAL INSTITUTE FOR TRIAL ADVOCACY

Address inquiries to:

Reprint Permission
National Institute for Trial Advocacy
1685 38th Street, Suite 200
Boulder, CO 80301-2735
Phone: (800) 225-6482
Fax: (720) 890-7069
E-mail: permissions@nita.org

ISBN 978-1-60156-214-2
FBA 1214

14 13 12 11 10 9 8 7 6 5 4 3 2 1
Printed in the United States of America

To Nina, Tori, Jeffrey, Annika, and Sonja.
Thank you for inspiring me and reminding me of those things that are important.

CONTENTS

EXHIBITS

INTRODUCTION

This is an action for eviction under Nita's public housing statutes. On Month-0, YR-0, Ladonna Johnson, her two grandchildren, and her great-grandchild received notice of eviction from Nita Gardens. Nita Gardens is Nita City's public housing project. The grounds for the eviction are violations of the lease, specifically § 8 Resident Obligations (C): "refrain from engaging in, and cause members of the resident's household, any guest, or any other person under resident's control to refrain from engaging in, any criminal or illegal activity including . . . any criminal, illegal or other activity which threatens the health, safety, or right to peaceful enjoyment of public housing premises by another NCHA resident or employee. . . ." Ten months before the eviction action Ms. Johnson's grandson, Elroy, along with several other young men, was arrested for possession and sale of crack cocaine. Elroy Johnson was charged, but the District Attorney later dropped the charges when Elroy agreed to testify against other defendants. Several of the others in the group were convicted. None of those who were convicted live at Nita Gardens. It is alleged that people with whom Elroy associates constitute a "criminal street gang" under Nita law and that Elroy Johnson is a gang member. Elroy Johnson's activities as a tagger are also alleged to be in violation of the lease.

Ms. Johnson claims her eviction is a result of her activism with other tenants at Nita Gardens. In Month-8, Ms. Johnson formed a Tenant Action Committee, whose specific purpose was to have fire sprinklers installed at Nita Gardens. Ms. Johnson had lost a family member to an apartment fire, and when new guidelines for fire safety were introduced by the Fire Protection League of Nita, she was adamant about the installation of sprinklers regardless of cost. The Tenant Action Committee was unable to persuade the building manager to ask the City of Nita to install a sprinkler system in the building. On Month-7, 13, and 20 the Tenant Action Committee held protests in the building. These tenant protests disrupted daily life at Nita Gardens. Ms. Johnson alleges her eviction is retaliation for her community activism and a violation of the terms of her lease.

The nature of eviction cases requires a short timeline for the action. To make this case as realistic as possible we partially deviate from the traditional NITA system of dating. Starting from the date set when you will try the case, those using the file should work backward by months. All factual dates in these materials are stated in the following form:

Month-0   represents the month of the trial;

Month-1   represents one month preceding;

Month-2   represents two months preceding;

YR-0   represents the actual year in which the case is being tried (i.e., the present year);

YR-1   represents last year (please use the actual year);

YR-2   represents the year before last (please use the actual year), etc.

STIPULATIONS

1. Nita Gardens is the only public housing in Nita City.

2. The Nita City Housing Authority and Nita Gardens are in compliance with all state and federal regulations regarding public housing.

3. The photographs and diagrams are accurate descriptions and depictions of what they represent on the dates in question.

4. Detective Behmer is unavailable to testify.

LANDLORD/TENANT COURT, COUNTY OF DARROW, STATE OF NITA
Case No. LTC-1087
SUMMONS IN EVICTION

NITA CITY HOUSING AUTHORITY
    Plaintiff,

v.

LADONNA JOHNSON
    Defendant.

To the above named Defendant: Take note that

1. On Wednesday, Month-3 28, YR-0, at 10:00 a.m., in the Nita City Landlord/Tenant Court, 687 Main Street, Nita City, Nita, the Court may be asked to enter judgment against you as set forth in the Complaint.

2. A copy of the Complaint against you and an Answer form that you must use if you file an Answer are attached.

3. If you do not agree with the Complaint, then you must either

    a. Go to the Court, located at 687 Main Street, Nita City, Nita, at the above date and time and file the Answer stating any legal reason you have why judgment should not be entered against you, or

    b. File the Answer with the Court before that date and time.

4. When you file your Answer, you must pay a filing fee to the Clerk of the Court.

5. If you file an Answer, you must give or mail a copy to the Plaintiff or the attorney who signed the Complaint.

6. If you do not file with the Court at or before the time for appearance specified in this Summons an Answer to the Complaint setting forth the grounds upon which you base your claim for possession and denying or admitting all of the material allegations of the Complaint, judgment by default may be taken against you for the possession of the property described in the Complaint; for the rent, if any due or to become due; for present and future damages; and for any other relief to which the Plaintiff is entitled.

7. If you want a jury trial, you must ask for one in the Answer and pay a jury fee in addition to the filing fee.

8. If you want to file an Answer or request a jury trial and you are indigent, you must appear at the above date and time, fill out a financial affidavit, and ask the Court to waive the fees.

Respectfully submitted this 1st day of Month-3, YR-0.

Susan Maranetty

Attorney for the Nita City Housing Authority

This summons is issued pursuant to Rule 303, Rules of Landlord/Tenant Court Civil Procedure, as amended, and 15-10-231, N.R.S. A copy of the Complaint must be served with this Summons. This form should be used only for actions filed under Nita's Landlord/Tenant Act. WARNING: All fees are nonrefundable. In some cases, a request for a jury trial may be denied pursuant to law even though a jury fee has been paid.

LANDLORD/TENANT COURT, COUNTY OF DARROW, STATE OF NITA
Case No. LTC-1087
VERIFIED COMPLAINT FOR EVICTION

NITA CITY HOUSING AUTHORITY
    Plaintiff,

v.

LADONNA JOHNSON
    Defendant.

The Plaintiff, through the attorney for Nita City Housing Authority, states as follows:

1. Plaintiff, the Nita City Housing Authority (NCHA), is the owner of the public housing development, Nita Gardens, located at 874 Jackson Avenue, Nita City, Nita, the legal description of which is to wit: Lot 1–5, Kolp Subdivision, County of Darrow, Nita City, State of Nita.

2. Plaintiff is a participant in the Federal Government Housing Program, commonly known as the Section 8 New Construction Program, and receives rental subsidies from the United States Department of Housing and Urban Development (hereinafter known as "HUD"). As such, Plaintiff must comply with 42 U.S.C. § 1437d (1994), The Anti-Drug Abuse Act of 1988.

3. Plaintiff leased the premises to Defendant pursuant to a HUD-approved written lease. Rent is due on the first day of each month. Monthly rental of said premises at this time payable by tenant is $169.00

4. Defendant entered into occupancy of said premises.

5. Defendant breached the terms of Paragraph 8 Resident Obligations section (C) of the lease by failing to refrain from engaging in, or causing members of the resident's household, guests, or other people under the resident's control to refrain from engaging in, any criminal or illegal activity. Specifically, involvement in any violent or drug-related criminal activity on or off NCHA property, membership in a criminal street gang, and defacing public property without the consent of the owner.

6. Plaintiff has elected to terminate said tenancy on Month-3, 30, YR-0.

7. A Ten-Day Lease Notice of Material Noncompliance and Demand for Possession as required by Defendant's lease and statute were served upon the Defendant on June 21, YR-0, by posting in a conspicuous place upon the premises, to wit: under the front door of Apartment 715-E, Nita Gardens, 874 Jackson Avenue, Nita City, Nita, and by mailing a copy of the same to said address on the same date.

8. Defendant failed to surrender possession of said premises and unlawfully, wrongly, and without force holds possession of the premises, contrary to the terms of the lease.

9. Defendant tendered the $169.00 tenant portion of rents to Plaintiff for June and July, which has been returned to the Defendant. The government subsidized rents for June and July are being held subsequent to resolution of the within action.

WHEREFORE, Plaintiff prays for recovery of possession of said premises, for judgment for rent due or to become due, present and future damages, attorneys fees, costs, and any other relief to which Plaintiff is entitled.

Dated this 1st Day of Month-3, YR-0.

Susan Maranetty

Attorney for the Nita City Housing Authority

Plaintiff's address:

Nita City Housing Authority
Legal Department
875 Main Street
AHEF-14
Nita City, Nita
555-423-6814

TEN-DAY LEASE NOTICE OF MATERIAL NONCOMPLIANCE*
and
STATUTORY NOTICE TO QUIT

(SUBSEQUENT BREACH FOR DRUG AND GANG RELATED ACTIVITY)

*WARNING: Pursuant to paragraph 9(B)(3) of your lease and federal regulations, HUD-required notice periods and notice periods required by State law may run concurrently. Therefore, no additional notices will be served upon you.

TO TENANT: Ladonna Johnson

ADDRESS: 874 Jackson Avenue, Apt. 715-E
Nita City, Nita

AND ALL OTHER OCCUPANTS OF THE PREMISES

Notice is hereby given that you have breached the covenants and conditions of Paragraphs 8(C)(2) and 9(B)(3) of the lease under which you hold possession of the above-described premises, and the Landlord proposes to terminate your lease for material noncompliance thereof, in the following particulars. On Month-10, 8, your grandson, Elroy Johnson, was arrested for the possession and sale of crack cocaine under N.R.S 18-12-893.13 Prohibited acts; penalties. He was charged with a felony under Nita law. He is also associated with individuals believed to be involved in a "criminal street gang" as defined under Nita Revised Statute 18-23-101 et seq. He has also participated in defacing public property through graffiti.

These are material breaches under 42 U.S.C. § 1437d(l)(6) (1994 ed., Supp. V), The Anti-Drug Abuse Act of 1988. The Act, as later amended, provides that "each public housing agency shall utilize leases which . . . provide that any criminal activity that threatens the health, safety, or right to peaceful enjoyment of the premises by other tenants or any drug-related criminal activity on or off such premises, engaged in by a public housing tenant, any member of the tenant's household, or any guest or other person under the tenant's control, shall be cause for termination of tenancy."

YOU ARE FURTHER NOTIFIED:

A. That Landlord of the above-described premises demands that you shall, within ten (10) days of the time this notice is served upon you, SURRENDER the possession of said premises that you occupy as tenant and that are known as Nita Gardens, 874 Jackson Avenue, Apartment 715-E, Nita City, Nita. This notice extends the statutory three-day Notice to Quit of N.R.S. Chapter 239 to ten days. No additional three-day Notice to Quit will be served.

B. You are hereby notified that your tenancy has been terminated on Month-3, 28, YR-0. The undersigned, as agent for the Landlord, demands that you shall deliver to the Landlord the possession of the Premises on or before that date and time, to wit: you must vacate by midnight on Month-3, 28, YR-0.

C. You have ten (10) days within which to discuss the proposed termination of your tenancy with the Landlord/Landlord's agent; the Landlord/Landlord's agent shall discuss this matter with you upon request.

D. If the Landlord commences an action to evict you, you have the right to defend the action in Court.

This demand is made pursuant to N.R.S. 13-40-106 et. seq. as a result of your subsequent breach of the same conditions of your lease and pursuant to HUD regulation.

Monthly rent at this time is $169.00 payable on the first day of each month.

Dated this 1st day of Month-3 YR-0.

Susan Maranetty

Attorney for Nita City Housing Authority

CERTIFICATE OF MAILING

I hereby certify that I mailed a true and correct copy of the foregoing TEN-DAY LEASE NOTICE OF MATERIAL NONCOMPLIANCE and STATUTORY NOTICE TO QUIT, by placing in the U.S. Mail postage prepaid, this 1st day of Month-3, YR-0, to:

Ladonna Johnson
874 Jackson Avenue, Apt. 715-E
Nita City, Nita 00251

Susan Maranetty

Attorney for Nita City Housing Authority

A posting of a true copy hereof was slipped under the door of the apartment.

NITA CITY HOUSING AUTHORITY
    Plaintiff,

v.

LADONNA JOHNSON
    Defendant.

The Defendant, Ladonna Johnson, by and through her attorney, Nita Legal Services, Inc. appearing, and as her answer to the Plaintiff's complaint states:

1. Defendant Ladonna Johnson admits items 1, 4, 6, and 9 of the complaint and denies items 5, 7, and 8 of the Complaint;

2. Plaintiff is not entitled to possession of the property, and Defendant is entitled to retain possession for the following reasons:

    a. Defendant's grandson, Elroy Johnson, was wrongly accused of possession and sale of crack cocaine. He was not convicted in this matter. Defendant is therefore not in violation of Paragraph 8(C)(2) of the lease;

    b. Defendant's grandson is not a member of a "criminal street gang." Defendant is therefore not in violation of Paragraph 8(A) or C(1);

    c. Defendant's grandson has not been convicted, or even charged with, defacing public property. Defendant is therefore not in violation of Paragraph 8(A).

    d. The Plaintiff's actions are retaliation, based on legal actions by the Defendant in forming a Tenant Action Committee in Month-8 for the purposes of persuading Nita Gardens or the City of Nita to install fire sprinklers in the halls, public areas, and residences of Nita Gardens. The Defendant is entitled to her actions under Paragraph 7(B) of the lease: "Not interfere with Resident's constitutional rights to organize/join a tenant organization." Plaintiff's actions are also in violation of Defendant's constitutional rights under the First Amendment of the U.S. Constitution.

WHEREFORE, Defendant prays for judgment that she is entitled to retain possession of Apartment 715-E, 874 Jackson Avenue, Nita City, Nita, and Plaintiff takes nothing by its Complaint.

The Defendant demands trial by jury.

CERTIFICATE OF MAILING

I certify that a true copy of the answer was mailed, postage prepaid, to:

Nita City Housing Authority
Legal Department
AHEF-14
875 Main Street
Nita City, Nita 00244

Dated this 8th day of Month-3, YR-0.

Nelson Ridgeway

Attorney, Nita Legal Services, Inc.

LANDLORD/TENANT COURT, COUNTY OF DARROW, STATE OF NITA
Case No. LTC-1087
MOTION TO PROCEED IN FORMA PAUPERIS

NITA CITY HOUSING AUTHORITY
    Plaintiff,

v.

LADONNA JOHNSON
    Defendant.

Defendant, LADONNA JOHNSON, through her attorneys, Nita Legal Services, Inc., moves to file her defense in this action without necessity of prepaying fees, pursuant to Chapter 221, N.R.S., for the reason that she is a poor person and unable to pay the costs and expenses thereof. As reason in support of her Motion, the Defendant states to the Court as follows:

1. The attached Affidavit [not included] of the Defendant indicates the Defendant is Indigent.

2. The Defendant has a meritorious claim.

3. Due to Defendant's financial circumstances, her inability to pay fees would preclude her from presenting her claims.

The Defendant respectfully requests that this Court allow her to file this action without the necessity of prepaying fees.

Respectfully submitted,

Nelson Ridgeway

Nita Legal Services, Inc.
Attorneys for Ladonna Johnson

LANDLORD/TENANT COURT, COUNTY OF DARROW, STATE OF NITA
Case No. LTC-1087
ORDER FOR LEAVE TO PROCEED IN FORMA PAUPERIS

NITA CITY HOUSING AUTHORITY
    Plaintiff,

v.

LADONNA JOHNSON
    Defendant.

THIS MATTER coming on to be heard upon Defendant to file her answer in this action without pre-payment of fees, and to have determination thereon;

AND the Court having considered the same, finding that she is a poor person and unable to pay said fees, and that her Petition appears meritorious;

IT IS THEREFORE ORDERED that the she be allowed to file her Answer in the above entitled action without the payment of fees pursuant to Chapter 221, N.R.S.

ORDERED this 8th day of Month-3, YR-0.

Robert McGladry, Jr

Robert L. McGladry, Jr.
Presiding Judge

LANDLORD/TENANT COURT, COUNTY OF DARROW, STATE OF NITA
Case No. LTC-1087
STIPULATED MOTION FOR CONTINUANCE

NITA CITY HOUSING AUTHORITY
    Plaintiff,

v.

LADONNA JOHNSON
    Defendant.

Come now the parties, by and through their attorneys of record and respectfully request that the trial in this matter, scheduled to begin on Month-3, 28, YR-0, be continued for no more than ninety days. As grounds for this stipulated motion, counsel state:

1. Trial on this eviction action is scheduled to begin on Month- 3, 28, YR-0.

2. Both parties believe that expert testimony is necessary in this case, given some unique issues.

3. While submission of expert testimony is unusual in case of this nature, both counsel agree that such testimony will assist the finder of fact in making decisions in this case and that allowing each side to present expert testimony will serve the interests of justice.

Wherefore, counsel stipulate that the trial in this case, scheduled to begin on

Month- 3, 28, YR-0, be vacated and that the Court reset this case for trial not more than ninety days from the present trial date.

Done this 12th day of Month-3, YR-0.

Susan Maranetty

Attorney for Plaintiff

Nelson Ridgeway

Attorney for Defendant

LANDLORD/TENANT COURT, COUNTY OF DARROW, STATE OF NITA
Case No. LTC-1087
ORDER RE: STIPULATED MOTION FOR CONTINUANCE

NITA CITY HOUSING AUTHORITY
    Plaintiff,

v.

LADONNA JOHNSON
    Defendant.

This matter comes on for consideration of the parties *Stipulated Motion for Continuance*, filed Month-3, 8, YR-0. Although the basis for the Motion is unusual, I find that the parties have demonstrated good cause for the requested continuance.

It is therefore **ORDERED** that the current trial date in this case, Month-3, 28, YR-0, be **VACATED** and that this matter is reset for trial on Month-0, 27, YR-0.

Done this 15th day of Month-3, YR-0.

Robert McGladry, Jr

Robert L. McGladry, Jr.
Presiding Judge

Statement of Rachel Longly

1   My name is Rachel Longly. I am the administrator/manager of Nita Gardens, Nita City's public
2   housing project. I have worked in this capacity for the past ten years.
3
4   I have a Bachelor of Arts degree, with a major in Political Science, from Nita State University.
5   I also have a master's degree in Business Management from Howard University, with a
6   concentration in public housing.
7
8   During my college years I volunteered with the NAACP, helping with voter registration
9   among other things. While in graduate school, I continued my work with voter registration in
10 Washington, DC. Doing voter registration was my inspiration for working in public housing.
11 I received an award from the NAACP during my last year at Howard as an Outstanding African-
12 American Woman.
13
14 Before I started with Nita City Housing Authority, I worked for the City of Pueblo, Colorado, in
15 their public housing department. I first worked in the main office as assistant to the director.
16 My job responsibilities included developing public policy, developing budgets, coordinating
17 contractors and scheduling major repairs in housing units, and acting as a liaison with building
18 managers. I worked in that office for approximately four years.
19
20 Approximately six months into my fourth year, I received a promotion to be manager for a
21 small housing unit. My responsibilities as manager included: negotiating leases with tenants;
22 collecting rents; enforcing housing authority rules, regulations, and policies; scheduling
23 repairs to units and the building in general; planning and maintaining a budget for the building;
24 complying with city, state, and federal regulations regarding health and funding; supervising a
25 staff that included an office clerk and maintenance workers; and serving as a contact with the
26 police, fire, and sanitation departments.
27
28 During the next four years I continued to be promoted until I was manager of Pueblo's largest
29 public housing development. I had been an administrator/manager of that building for
30 two years when I accepted my current position with Nita City Housing Authority.
31
32 My job description for Nita Gardens is substantially similar to that of my last position in
33 Colorado.
34
35 The biggest difference is that Nita Gardens is a much larger facility, and my staff is four times
36 as large.
37
38 Nita Gardens is a large public housing development. The building houses 350 variously-sized
39 apartments.
40
41 The building is configured into four wings: north, south, east, and west. The building has nine
42 stories, of which eight are for apartments. There is a laundry room on each floor in each wing,

1 for a total of thirty-two laundry rooms. The main floor houses offices, a mail room, a large
2 public meeting room, several all-purpose meeting and class rooms, a simple gymnasium that
3 has some fitness equipment, a basketball court, and a volleyball court.
4
5 Residents of the building are all on public assistance. They pay on a sliding scale that is based
6 on their income or level of public assistance. We have people of all ages living in the building,
7 from babies to senior citizens. We have tenants who live by themselves and families of up
8 to ten people. The building is an ethnic and religious melting pot. In short, we have a lot
9 of diversity. This is both good and bad. I like seeing people of all races and religions living
10 together, as it promotes a good living environment. It can also be a big problem as we try
11 to cater to such a wide variety of tastes; we simply can't please every person all of the time.
12 I can't tell you how many times I have acted as referee to try to help tenants settle disputes.
13 Sometimes I just have to get tough and tell people what they must do to solve a problem. It's
14 those times when I'm not a very popular person. Otherwise, I would say the tenants like and
15 respect me.
16
17 Crime can be an issue in our building. Nita Gardens is located in what could be described
18 as a "rough" part of town. We are constantly combating street-gang activity. This includes
19 everything from our constant battle with removing graffiti to working with the police and
20 drug enforcement agencies to stop drug sales. We regularly deal with many types of violence,
21 including domestic and child abuse, assaults, and the occasional rape. Fortunately, we have
22 never had a murder at Nita Gardens. We employ security officers and have a security team
23 on-site twenty four hours a day, seven days a week. Our goal is to protect our tenants and
24 maintain a safe and happy environment. It doesn't always work, but we try hard to keep crime
25 from taking root.
26
27 We constantly monitor a group of young men and women who call themselves the Vice Lords.
28 They began making use of our parking lot as a place to congregate after Elroy Johnson invited
29 them. They also make use of our recreational facilities as a couple of their members live in
30 the complex. We do our best to discourage them from using our facilities and loitering in our
31 parking lot. It is difficult when a resident invites them onto our property. Frankly, residents are
32 intimidated by this group. They scare me. I do not want to have to deal with the fallout when
33 someone gets seriously injured.
34
35 Tenants in our building do receive a wide variety of federal subsidies. Others receive subsidies
36 from the State of Nita. Virtually everyone in the building receives some type of grant in aid to
37 help pay for their housing. Because of this, we must be sure that we comply with federal and
38 state law relating to funding. One of the most difficult but important laws we must enforce
39 is the Anti-Drug Abuse Act of 1988. This law means that Nita Gardens has to include in our
40 lease a provision that says that criminal activity that threatens the health, safety, or right to
41 peaceful enjoyment of the premises by other tenants, or any drug-related criminal activity on
42 or off such premises, shall be cause for termination of the tenancy. This is particularly strict
43 because it covers behavior both on and off our premises and a wide range of people. This
44 includes tenants, any member of the tenant's household, or any guest or other person under
45 the tenant's control. To maintain our funding stream we must take an aggressive position on

1 any criminal or drug activities. The tenants know about this policy, and I think most of them
2 support it. Probably a couple of times each year we terminate a lease as a result of violating
3 this policy.
4
5 I do know Ladonna Johnson. She has lived at Nita Gardens with her two grandchildren and
6 great grandchild for about five years. I like and respect Ladonna. She is a no-nonsense type of
7 person who stands up for what she thinks is right. She is good with the children in the building,
8 and many call her Gram. Most of the time she was a quiet tenant who was respected, and she
9 lived by our rules. It is a sad situation that we have to evict her. In some sense, she is a victim
10 of our anti-drug policy. Her grandson, Elroy, runs with the Vice Lords. Many of the boys in the
11 group have been in trouble with the police. I know of two other boys who live in the building.
12 Most of the group does not live here, and until Elroy Johnson invited them onto the property,
13 they stayed away. As soon as Elroy became involved they started to hang out in our public
14 rooms or out in our parking lot. It all started in the fall of YR-1. All of a sudden I started seeing
15 Vice Lords in our gym. Elroy Johnson was playing basketball with them. It was pretty clear to
16 me he had invited them. Frankly, it's the outsiders who make the most trouble. They are the
17 ones who got Elroy in trouble. In Month-10 the police caught the group selling crack cocaine
18 out in our parking lot. They arrested the whole group for possession and sale. I'm not sure of
19 Elroy's status. I know he was arrested, but I do not know if he was convicted of anything. It
20 really didn't matter.
21
22 Our policy is pretty clear—get caught committing a crime or being involved in criminal drug
23 activity and you and your family are out of Nita Gardens. This one action, combined with his
24 association with gang activities, is sufficient. Because of Elroy's actions, the Johnson family has
25 not refrained from activities that threaten the health, safety, or right to peaceful enjoyment of
26 Nita Gardens. It's a shame that Ms. Johnson, her granddaughter, and her great-granddaughter
27 are being put out for Elroy's folly. My hands are tied; we must enforce our policies. If not, it
28 would be anarchy here at Nita Gardens. I will not let street gang bullies intimidate me or the
29 residents of this building.
30
31 We have very rarely evicted someone for a single violation of the "criminal drug activity"
32 provision of the lease. We have not invoked the clause for simple misdemeanor convictions
33 based on possession.
34
35 However, we do place closer scrutiny on people convicted for simple possession—where
36 there is smoke, there is fire. There have been a number of situations where there were single
37 allegations of serious criminal activity, such as the sale of drugs, but no conviction. We have
38 not evicted in those situations. We have employed the clause for both drug convictions
39 and other serious criminal activity such as assault, domestic abuse, and rape. The reason
40 we decided to employ the clause for the Johnson family was because we believe Elroy has
41 attracted a street gang into the complex. The drug arrests last year were the first time the
42 police made any arrests tied to drug and gang activity on our property.
43
44 Clearly, this is interfering with other residents' rights to health, safety, and peaceful enjoyment
45 of Nita Gardens.

1   I did have a series of encounters with Ms. Johnson that weren't especially pleasant. These
2   encounters occurred in Month-8 and continued for the next few months. It began when
3   Ladonna came to my office for a meeting. She demanded that we install a sprinkler system
4   for both common areas and all residences. She brought with her documents someone had
5   downloaded from the Internet, including something from the Nita Fire Department. Installing
6   sprinklers in our building is an unreasonable demand that she pushed to the extreme.
7
8   We always do our best to meet and exceed government requirements for safety. Every part of
9   the building currently meets standards for fire safety. I know there are attempts being made to
10   require public housing to retrofit existing buildings with sprinkler systems. Some proponents
11   want to have hallways and public areas fitted with sprinkler systems. Others want both public
12   and living areas to have fire safety systems. Our building is older, having been built in the late
13   1960s. When it was built, it was state-of-the-art for public housing. Over the years standards
14   have changed. New public buildings have far stricter safety standards, especially for fires. Nita
15   Gardens does not have a sprinkler system, either in public or private areas. We have installed
16   smoke detectors in all public areas, including the main floor, hallways, and laundry rooms. We
17   offer residents a substantial discount to purchase battery-powered smoke detectors for their
18   apartments. The city has investigated the costs of installing sprinklers in Nita Gardens and
19   found the costs would be excessive to retrofit the building. It would cost over a million dollars
20   to make these changes, and we would have to close the building for more than six months to
21   have a system installed. The building is reaching the end of its useful life, and the city does
22   not want to make substantial investments in a building slated for demolition within the next
23   ten years.
24
25   Ms. Johnson did not feel the same way. Because her daughter died in an apartment fire she
26   was rabid about fire safety. She was petrified that a building fire would kill her granddaughter
27   or great-granddaughter.
28
29   She came to me and demanded that we install a new fire safety system that included sprinklers,
30   smoke and carbon monoxide detectors, and voice alarms in each apartment. I told her the
31   costs of installing such a system would be enormous and it did not make economic sense to
32   make capital improvements in such an old building. I explained to her that the building was
33   in compliance with all parts of city, state, and federal fire codes. I showed her the emergency
34   plans for evacuating the building. I reminded her about our program to provide low-cost
35   smoke alarms to any resident who wished to purchase them. I even offered to hold fire drills
36   and fire safety programs for residents. She would have no part of my offers—it was refit the
37   building, period.
38
39   Ms. Johnson went out and formed a "Tenant Action Committee" for the sole purpose of forcing
40   the city to install a new fire safety system in the building. The action committee presented
41   me with a petition in Month 8 to have a system installed. When I told them I would not
42   bend to their demands, they started public protests. The group, led by Ms. Johnson, would
43   congregate on the main floor with big signs. They would chant, "Don't let my baby burn."
44   On a couple of occasions when I was present at the demonstrations, I had to have security
45   disperse the group. Ms. Johnson was clearly the leader, and security went to her first to get the

1 group to disband. The two most disruptive demonstrations occurred on Month-7, 13 and 20.
2 During this time we had an increase in false fire alarms. I'm not making any accusations, but
3 the coincidence seemed clear. We still have no plans to install sprinkler systems. Except for
4 Ms. Johnson, most tenants have moved beyond this issue.
5
6 I do not hold Ms. Johnson's activism against her. She is entitled to her own opinions and to voice
7 them through any tenant committee. Our policies and leases are quite clear that we do not
8 retaliate against tenants for their activism—even if it is a problem for building administration.
9 It is neither the building's policy nor my personal belief that we should hold a person's beliefs
10 against them. Ms. Johnson's eviction is based solely on her grandson's violation of Paragraph
11 8 of our lease. It is simply a coincidence the eviction was filed six months after her last protest.
12
13 I was contacted by the police on Month-10, 8, and was informed they were planning a large
14 arrest in the Nita Gardens parking lot. They told me they suspected our parking lot was being
15 used as a place to sell drugs and conduct other criminal activity. I let them know our security
16 officers would be available to assist if needed. I also told them I would be on the premises
17 that evening to make sure our tenants were safe. At approximately 7:30 p.m., a member of
18 our security force told me the police were in our parking lot. I immediately went out to the
19 parking lot to observe what was happening.
20
21 When I got out to the parking lot, I saw a whole fleet of police vehicles. They were surrounding
22 a group of men and women. I clearly saw Elroy Johnson in the group, but did not see Jimmy
23 Vasquez.
24
25 Elroy was in handcuffs and was being led to a police van.
26
27 Later, I spoke with Detective Behmer about the arrests. She gave me a list of all of those who
28 had been arrested. The list included Elroy Johnson. This was the last straw for me. Not only
29 had Elroy invited those thugs into Nita Gardens, but now they were selling drugs.
30
31 On another occasion I spoke with Lieutenant Wherder, the head of the Gang Task Force,
32 about the graffiti being painted on our building. He assured me that it was not gang related,
33 but the work of a gang of taggers. He told me he thought it was the work of a group called
34 Modern Neighborhood Art. He also told me he believed Elroy Johnson was involved with that
35 group. I have suspicions he is at the heart of defacing our building.
36
37 Whether he is a member of the Vice Lords or Modern Neighborhood Art, he is still in a gang.
38
39 I believe the gang members would not have been in the Nita Gardens parking lot but for the
40 invitation of Elroy Johnson and maybe Jimmy Vasquez. Elroy's connection to those who were
41 later convicted of drug charges is enough to trigger the clause in Ladonna Johnson's lease.
42 Before we commenced the eviction I spoke with the Nita City Attorney about the Johnson
43 lease. I wanted to be clear that the lease gave us the right to evict the Johnson family because
44 a member of the family had engaged in criminal activity that threatened the health, safety,
45 and right to peaceful enjoyment of our building. I am aware of the clause in our lease about

1   retaliation of tenant activities and that an eviction within six months of any tenant activity is
2   suspect. She confirmed my opinion that Elroy Johnson's activities were sufficient to trigger an
3   eviction regardless of Ladonna Johnson's tenant activities. It was because of those assurances
4   that I commenced the eviction.

Rachel Longly

Rachel Longly
Month-4, YR-0

STATEMENT OF ERNEST COMSTOCKE

1 My name is Ernest Comstocke. Some people call me "Deacon" because of my religious beliefs.
2 I head the maintenance team at Nita Gardens Public Housing. I've held the job for about ten
3 years and have worked at the complex for more than fifteen years. I report directly to Rachel
4 Longly. I have a crew of ten people who work with me to keep the building clean and in good
5 repair.
6
7 Besides supervising the maintenance and cleaning crew I also work around the building. I'm
8 good with my hands and can fix most anything if you give me enough time. Four of my crew
9 work full-time on cleaning. They maintain the common areas, including the first floor, the
10 halls, and the laundry rooms. Two of the crew are assigned to painting. Mostly these two deal
11 with graffiti painted by the local kids and gangs. We have a big problem with people painting
12 gang signs on the building. My rule is that any graffiti must be covered within twenty-four
13 hours. We don't want any of those punks to think they own any part of our building. Two
14 more employees work on maintenance. They do everything from clearing the garbage chutes
15 to patching pavement in the parking lot. The other two employees are assigned to maintain
16 the HVAC, or the building's heat and air conditioning systems. It's a pretty big job to keep the
17 building's systems working on a twenty-four hour basis. We pride ourselves in keeping Nita
18 Gardens in good shape—even if the building is getting to be an old lady.
19
20 I work twelve-hour shifts four days each week and am "on call" for the other three days.
21 When I'm on call, I carry a beeper and a cell phone. If necessary, I come to the building to
22 assist with emergency repairs or other issues. Because I work long hours, I know quite a few
23 of the people who live in the building—either by name or by recognition. I know "Gram"
24 Johnson. She's a pretty cool old gal. I see her around the building quite a bit when she isn't
25 working. She's real good with the kids and the young mothers. She takes quite a few under
26 her wing and helps them learn about taking care of their house and their kids. She'll tell you
27 straight to your face what she thinks. I like that in a person, 'cause I know exactly where they
28 stand. She and I are in agreement about kids. She wants no part of gangs. I know it breaks
29 her heart that her grandson hangs with the crowd that acts like they own our parking lot. I've
30 helped the security guards chase those punks on more than one occasion.
31
32 Gram is real serious about fire safety. I know her daughter was killed in a fire. The rumor is
33 she was smoking in bed and passed out due to drugs. Ms. Johnson is always after the cleaning
34 crew to empty the trash bins in the common areas, laundry, and trash rooms. She bugs the
35 maintenance guys about clearing clogs in the trash chutes. I would say she makes more
36 complaints than any other resident in the building. Sometimes she can be a real problem
37 with her complaints, especially when they take crews away from scheduled work. That really
38 disrupts the whole maintenance plan. That's when I get upset. Fortunately, Gram has only
39 done that a couple of times over the past few years.
40
41 Gram Johnson certainly did stir things up with her protests about a sprinkler system. While she
42 was always a bit over the top about fire safety, she really pushed things starting in Month-8.

1　She cornered me one morning and told me the building needed a sprinkler system. She told
2　me she had been to a presentation at the fire department and that they had showed her how
3　a fire prevention system would save lives and property. She told me she was going to make
4　sure Nita Gardens got its own fire system. I told her it would be almost impossible to install a
5　system without moving people out of the building and tearing up the place for months. She
6　didn't want to hear anything about time, costs, or disruption. I know she met with Ms. Longly
7　on the same subject in Month-8. Ms. Longly also tried to discourage Gram. I guess all she did
8　was to make her angry. Next thing I know these signs appeared all over the building. Then
9　in Month-7 the protests started. On Month-7, 13 and 20 a couple hundred people appeared
10　in the main lobby. They were carrying big signs and shouting things about the building being
11　unsafe. I took exception to those comments as everything is up to code and follows what is
12　required.
13
14　The second protest was bigger and louder than the first. Ms. Longly lost her temper and asked
15　security to break things up. She said if they couldn't get it done she would call the police. I saw
16　Gram Johnson at the protests. It was clear she was the leader. The day after, I told her she had
17　made a big mistake by organizing a protest. She let me know she was just exercising her rights
18　as a tenant and that she would do what it took to get a sprinkler system. Christmas came and
19　went, and the people in the building lost interest. I don't mind people asking for those things
20　they are entitled to receive. I do mind when it disrupts other people's lives. Gram Johnson
21　crossed that line with those protests.
22
23　I know both Sara and Elroy Johnson as well. Sara is a nice girl, and her baby is a real cutie. I know
24　Sara had her baby out of wedlock. Everyone, but a drug pusher, is entitled to a mistake. I think
25　it taught her a lesson about life, and now she is a good church-going woman.
26
27　Elroy is a different matter. He's a smart boy, but he is always into something that is trouble.
28　I admit I don't like him or trust him. When he first moved in, I caught him writing on a wall of
29　the building next door with a big marking pen. He was doing some kind of "word art" thing.
30　He was writing with a big marker, and I took the pen from him. I told him if I ever caught him
31　writing on the walls of Nita Gardens or any place else, I would tell his Gram and she would
32　deal with him, and then I'd get him thrown out of the building. Since then he has gotten real
33　smart.
34
35　I never see him with paint or markers, but I know he and his friends are behind the graffiti
36　that gets painted on our building. I just can't prove it. I also yell at him and some of the other
37　kids for riding their skateboards in the building. I don't mind if they ride outside, but it really
38　messes up the floors and the railings the way they ride in the building. Besides, it's just not
39　safe. Some day one of them will run into one of the older tenants, and then there will be real
40　trouble.
41
42　The building has a strict policy on graffiti. By law my crew must remove graffiti within twenty-
43　four hours of when it is discovered. We usually beat this limit because it really bothers me
44　to see the building defaced. If I catch the little creeps writing on the building I make them
45　clean it off and then call the cops. We get two kinds of writing on the building. The first type

1   is that fancy, pretty kind of street art. Big letters with spray paint filling stuff in. The subject
2   of that type of graffiti is usually something political—you know, "save the whales" or some
3   other liberal message. It's much harder to remove this stuff because it's really big, and they
4   often paint it on a surface that is hard to reach. Those are the ones I hate the most, but they
5   are also the ones the police say are less dangerous. There is a different type of graffiti as well.
6   It's usually done in those wide permanent markers. It's like some kind of code. You can tell
7   because some people either laugh or get angry when they see it. The ones that get people
8   most upset are things like "187" and then a list of names like Smiley, Flaco, Goofy, or Dog. The
9   police tell me this is some kind of a threat. Other times the graffiti is words like "Lords" or
10 "T-Birds" and some numbers and crude drawings like pitchforks, stars, and moons. When we
11 find this kind of graffiti we get rid of it as quickly as we can. The police tell us that if we paint
12 over graffiti immediately it is less likely taggers will use that spot again.
13
14 There are some pretty tough characters that live in the neighborhood. Most of the young men
15 and women who live in the building are decent people. It's the ones who are members of the
16 group they call the Vice Lords who are the bad ones. They act pretty tough. I know many of
17 the older residents are frightened when those hoods hang around. Most of them don't live in
18 our building, thank goodness.
19
20 Elroy Johnson and Jimmy Vasquez are the only building residents that I know who hang
21 out with those punks. I can't say that they are definitely gang members. I do know that the
22 Johnson boy was arrested in that big drug bust in Month-10. I see him around the building, so
23 I guess he got off. It doesn't matter much because his family is now being evicted. We don't
24 need that kind of bad influence living in our building. Whether he was doing drugs or not, he
25 invited those gang members to hang out in our parking lot and use our gym.
26
27 I don't always agree with Ms. Longly's enforcement of the drug use/criminal acts part of the
28 lease. There have been times when someone who got arrested for doing drugs didn't get
29 evicted. There have been times when the police arrested someone for beating their spouse
30 or kid, and they didn't get evicted. That sounds like she is being pretty selective about using
31 that clause. I think we should always evict a tenant who breaks the law.

Ernest Comstocke

Ernest Comstocke
Month-4, YR-0

STATEMENT OF JAMES WHERDER

1   My name is James Wherder. I'm a lieutenant for the Nita City Police Department currently
2   assigned to the Gang Task Force. I've been a police officer for my entire career, including
3   time served in the United States Army as a military police officer. I joined the Nita City Police
4   Department in the spring of YR-20. While I am peripherally connected to this case through
5   my command of the Gang Task Force, I specifically have been asked to serve as an expert
6   witness in this case. I have an opinion as to whether tagging done by Elroy Johnson creates an
7   atmosphere at Nita Gardens that threatens the health, safety, or right to peaceful enjoyment
8   of public housing residents.
9

10   After graduating from the police academy, I was assigned to street patrol in the inner city. As
11   a street officer, I developed a good rapport with many people on my beat. I also began a life-
12   long interest in the culture of street gangs. Five years ago I earned a Masters of Arts degree in
13   Anthropology from the University of Nita. My thesis was on the use of graffiti by urban gangs.
14   Obviously, my experience in the police force and work on the Gang Task Force helped me in
15   my research and writing. My other education is related to criminology with both an Associate
16   and BS degree in Criminology.
17

18   I have received four meritorious citations for my work in the inner city community. In YR-15
19   I received a citation for valor for stopping a liquor store robbery, where I was wounded in the
20   process of subduing two suspects. I knew both of the boys who committed that robbery. They
21   had just joined a gang, and the robbery was part of their initiation. I killed one of them, and
22   the other is still serving time. It was this action that led me to work on the Gang Task Force
23   and begin my academic studies.
24

25   Much of my work on the Gang Task Force now relates to the study and interpretation of graffiti.
26   Many people mistake all graffiti as gang related. This is not true. While street gangs do make
27   use of graffiti to mark territory, threaten individuals and other gangs, communicate with each
28   other, or even to show worthiness to join a specific gang, some groups of graffiti writers are
29   incorrectly identified as street gangs. They are more accurately referred to as tagging crews.
30   These groups have different motivations for creating graffiti. Just the same, these tagging
31   activities are also criminal in nature and have an effect on the public's perception of safety.
32

33   Graffiti, whether by members of a street gang or a tagger crew, is a means of marking territory.
34   Gangs leave their identification on fences, schools, sidewalks, walls, and even private homes.
35   Primary gang hangouts are often heavily covered with graffiti, including buildings and street
36   signs. Typically, graffiti includes the name of the gang, nicknames of the members of the
37   gang, slogans or symbols exclusive to the gang, the territory claimed, and even the names of
38   affiliated gangs. Sometimes gang graffiti presents threats or challenges to rival gangs or shows
39   disrespect for rivals. This type of graffiti often provokes confrontations and violence. This is
40   one of the reasons why we work hard to clean up graffiti, as it often multiplies as rivals cross
41   out and add their own messages.

1   Street gangs use their own language to communicate through graffiti. This language includes
2   numbers, letters, words, and phrases that are easily understood on the streets. The name of
3   the gang is often an abbreviation of two or three letters. Numbers have significant meaning in
4   graffiti. For example, the numbers 187 represent the California penal code section for murder.
5   Graffiti that includes those numbers is a death threat. Other numbers may represent the
6   number of a letter in the alphabet that is the first letter of the gang's name. Numbers may
7   also represent the street number for the location of where the gang was founded. Direction
8   coordinates such as E/S or W/S will show gang territory.
9
10 Graffiti is used to intimidate people, and it often makes local residents believe they are not
11 safe. It reduces the value of business and residential property and, left unchecked, may result
12 in a violent confrontation. Gang members view the messages left in graffiti as quite serious,
13 and the longer graffiti remains, the greater the chance of a violent confrontation. As part of
14 my work in preparing my opinion, I visited Nita Gardens and spoke with residents about their
15 feelings on graffiti. Many of those I spoke with indicated graffiti gave them a sense of being
16 violated. They were intimidated by the fact that someone came and wrote on the walls of
17 their homes. Many of the residents clearly feel threatened by having their home defaced.
18 One or two residents confided in me that they avoid those areas of Nita Gardens that have
19 been tagged in the past. Many feel threatened by the appearance of any type of graffiti and
20 no longer feel safe in their own homes. I showed a number of residents examples of graffiti
21 that appear in the area around Nita Gardens. They could not distinguish between true gang
22 markings and the writings of taggers.
23
24 A tagger gang is often smaller than the typical street gang. A typical tagger gang may have as few
25 as three or as many as ten members. Street gangs often recruit members of tagging crews to
26 write graffiti for them. Sometimes these people are gang members, and sometimes they are paid
27 or threatened to write for a street gang. The Nita City police department has not made tagging
28 a priority offense. Because we are under a shrinking budget due to the economic downturn,
29 emphasis is placed on more violent gang activities. Most tagging crews avoid violence, although
30 many taggers may become violent when caught and confronted by residents.
31
32 I am very well acquainted with the Vice Lords street gang. The members of that gang are
33 some very tough individuals and are considered by the Nita City Police Department to be
34 one of the worst street gangs in the state. They are loosely affiliated with a national street
35 gang. They are probably the Gang Units most active concern. In terms of criminal activity,
36 the Vice Lords have been connected with manufacturing and distributing crack cocaine. They
37 are also under investigation for extortion and prostitution. Vice Lords members are regularly
38 arrested for assault, petty theft, and alcohol-related crimes. A number of their members
39 have been convicted of serious crimes, including murder and rape. They are some very bad
40 people. I spend about 60 percent of my time working on matters related to the Vice Lords.
41 This includes work in the schools and on the streets trying to keep younger children from
42 becoming involved with the Vice Lords and their activities. The Vice Lords do make use of
43 graffiti as a means of marking their territory and threatening others. All of the Vice Lord
44 graffiti I encountered was similar to what I previously described as gang tagging.

1   I cannot say that every member of the Vice Lords is a truly bad actor. The Vice Lords work hard
2   to recruit new members. There is a great deal of pressure on the streets to force young men
3   and women who live in the area of Jackson Avenue and Twentieth Street to join the gang. It
4   takes real courage not to join the gang if you are a young man living in the heart of Vice Lords
5   territory. Most do not choose to say no to joining the gang because life as a teenager outside
6   the gang is quite difficult and perhaps even dangerous.
7
8   I suspect Elroy Johnson is the leader of the tagger gang MNA. This is one of the up-and-
9   coming groups of writers in Nita City. They have grown from being a local nuisance to gaining
10   citywide notoriety. There are some people, such as Professor Stockbridge, who call these
11   vandals "Urban Artists." In my opinion they are still common criminals. They take serious risks
12   in choosing their targets and drive many of us in the department crazy—not to mention the
13   Department of Sanitation and private citizens who have to paint over their work. I admit we
14   have put a priority on street gang crime. Just the same, the vandalism of graffiti is still a crime.
15   Graffiti is prohibited by a city ordinance, not a state statute. That's the main reason we devote
16   more time to the higher level crimes of street gangs. If the city would increase my budget,
17   we would certainly devote more effort to controlling the activities of tagger gangs. There will
18   come a day when MNA goes too far, and we will have to put them out of business.
19
20   I am aware that Professor Stockbridge calls the graffiti done by MNA "Urban Art." My research
21   in this case shows the residents of Nita Gardens do not distinguish between gang graffiti and
22   tagger writing. Many residents perceive graffiti as an attack on the person in the same way as
23   an actual physical touching. By having a place where they live defaced, some residents feel
24   as if they have been personally accosted, and they are afraid their physical person will be
25   next. It is similar to how people feel when an individual breaks into their property and steals
26   something. There is a loss of trust in the safety of their home.
27
28   If we catch Elroy Johnson and his crew actually defacing property, we will arrest and prosecute
29   them. At the present time we have never arrested or convicted Elroy Johnson for tagging. Do
30   I know he is a tagger? Yes. Can I prove it? No. Can I say he is a member of the Vice Lords? No,
31   I have no clear proof Elroy Johnson is a member of that street gang. He does spend time with
32   members of the gang—so guilt by association. I know that some gangs hire taggers to write
33   their graffiti for them. I have never connected Elroy Johnson to Vice Lord graffiti, but I also
34   cannot say he has not done work for hire.
35
36   I was not specifically involved in the operation of Month-10, where my unit arrested a number
37   of minors and adults for the possession and sale of crack cocaine. The arrests were based on
38   reports from residents of Nita Gardens and others in the area around that complex. These
39   reports placed gang members either on the premises of Nita Gardens or in the parking lot
40   of the complex for the purpose of selling illegal drugs. The arrests were part of an ongoing
41   investigation targeting the Vice Lords as one of the largest distributors of cocaine in Nita
42   City. That campaign continues today. We have been successful in many of our efforts as our
43   investigations have culminated in a series of arrests and convictions throughout Nita City.
44   The arrests at Nita Gardens were targeted for Month-10, 8. Twenty arrests were made in that

1   operation. I consider this campaign very successful as we were able to get five convictions. It

2   put a serious dent in the Vice Lords's drug operations for a number of months.

3

4   I was not on duty when the arrests were made at Nita Gardens on Month 10, 8. This operation

5   was under the direction of a different officer who was under my command. The operational

6   commander decided to arrest all of those who were congregating in the parking lot. As it

7   turned out, that was a good decision, because we netted a number of serious criminals in that

8   group. We also caught a break, because we were able to persuade some of those caught in

9   the roundup to testify against others. This included Elroy Johnson.

10

11   You have asked for my professional opinion on whether the painting or writing of graffiti on

12   public and private surfaces creates an environment that threatens the health, safety, or right

13   to peaceful enjoyment of the residents of Nita Gardens. There has been no showing that Nita

14   Gardens invited anyone to place graffiti or urban art on the building. Clearly, this uninvited

15   defacing of the building causes residents to feel unsafe. I support the building in its efforts to

16   remove a threat to its residents through the eviction of the Johnson family. The work of Elroy

17   Johnson and his tagging gang violates the law and places the residents of Nita Gardens in a

18   state of fear for their health and safety.

James Wherder
Month-1, YR-0

ADDITIONAL STATEMENT OF JAMES WHERDER

1 Since I initially offered my opinion there have been some changes in circumstances regarding
2 Elroy Johnson.
3
4 In the fall of YR-1, I began a program designed as an intervention for troubled youth in Nita
5 City. The program is called GRASP, or Gang Rescue and Support Project. GRASP's goal is to
6 get inner city youngsters who are gang members or who are flirting with gang involvement
7 to put their energy into other activities. The program has a three-pronged approach; the
8 first addresses both body and mind. The department offers a number of sports programs
9 that give troubled young men and women an outlet for their frustrations. By working with
10 trained officers and volunteers, we help these young people burn off aggression and energy.
11 The second prong offers help with school assignments. We have a team of volunteer tutors
12 who work to help keep these kids in school by showing them they can be successful. The
13 third prong is a program to divert taggers. We have those who have either been convicted
14 of tagging or who we suspect of being part of tagging gangs paint murals in areas that are
15 hotbeds for tagging. The first mural we did was an attempt to create a ceasefire between
16 rival gangs. It was very successful both in calming tensions and diverting taggers into what
17 Professor Stockbridge calls Urban Art.
18
19 This third prong has drawn lots of attention to the program in the media. Reports from both
20 Nita stations and from a number of radio and television networks covered the work of our
21 young "artists."
22
23 Elroy Johnson is now a member of GRASP. He came by the Gang Unit and said he wanted to
24 be involved with our next mural. You may have seen the photograph of Elroy painting part of
25 a new mural that is being done on Jackson Street. I admit he is pretty good with a can of spray
26 paint. The mural is looking good, and Elroy contributed a great deal towards its design and
27 completion. He was able to get a number of his friends to participate in painting the mural.
28 Perhaps it is just a coincidence, but since Elroy joined GRASP and started painting the mural
29 there have been no instances of MNA graffiti found in Nita City.
30
31 I'm not sure of the Johnson boy's intentions. I know his grandmother is being evicted from Nita
32 Gardens and there is a connection between her eviction, Elroy's arrest, and his connection to
33 MNA. My personal feeling is he is doing this as a means of saving his grandmother's lease. If
34 he stays part of GRASP after this case is over then I will be a believer. Until then, I am skeptical
35 of his motives.

James Wherder

James Wherder
Month-0, 3, YR-0

STATEMENT OF LADONNA JOHNSON

1   My name is Ladonna Johnson. I'm sixty-six years old. I currently live at Nita Gardens apartments
2   with my two grandchildren and my great-granddaughter. I've lived at Nita Gardens for the
3   past five years. I live there because I can't afford to live anywhere else.
4
5   I work part-time as a cook for Tender Years Day Care. It gives me a little money, and I love
6   working with all the babies. They are so special and cute. They just make me smile all the
7   time! I've been a cook all my life. I've worked at lots of restaurants all over Nita City. About
8   six years ago I got burned real bad on my legs when a hot kettle of soup spilled on me. I can't
9   work full time anymore. Because I can't work much I receive money from the government to
10   help me get along. That's why I live at Nita Gardens—I get money to help me pay the rent,
11   and I receive food stamps.
12
13   Like I said, I live with my two grandchildren and great-granddaughter. The kids live with me
14   because their mother passed away. My daughter was a good soul, but she couldn't stay off
15   the bottle and drugs. She died in a fire in her apartment. The fire department said she had
16   been smoking in bed and passed out from the alcohol and drug intoxication. Nobody should
17   die that way, and now I do everything I can to make sure it's safe where I live. I want to protect
18   those children!
19
20   My granddaughter's name is Sara. She is eighteen years old and still in school. I want her to
21   get her high school degree so she can have a good life. Sara is a bit like her mother. She got
22   in with the wrong crowd a couple of years ago, and some boy got her with child. That young
23   man wouldn't step up and take responsibility. He just split, and we never see him around.
24   Somebody's got to take care of that child, so I do my best until Sara finishes school. I just love
25   that baby. Anna is her name.
26
27   My grandson, Elroy, he's sixteen. He's a pretty good boy, but I worry he spends too much time
28   with bad boys and girls. I'm always after that boy to get himself together. I've got to ride him
29   hard to make sure he does what is right. He's not very good at most school subjects, except
30   art and sports. I think he believes he can make a living being a basketball star. I keep telling
31   him he's got to do more than play hoops to make his way in the world. I think he'll be all right.
32   He has some talent as an artist. He is always drawing and making pretty pictures out of words.
33   After he got in trouble in Month-10, he's pretty scared of the police. Some other boys went to
34   jail over that mess, and I know Elroy doesn't want to do time and ruin his life. Elroy got himself
35   into a tight spot in Month-10. He was hanging out with some other boys. If you ask me, some
36   of those boys are gang wannabes. They try to act real tough and talk with no respect.
37
38   Some of those boys I just don't like. Well, this group likes to hang out after school, in the
39   evening, and on weekends. They play basketball in our gym and mostly stand around outside
40   the building. Last January, Elroy was out in the parking lot with his friends. Next thing everyone
41   knows there were flashing lights and sirens. The cops came and arrested them all, even Elroy,
42   for dope. I say the only dope was Elroy for getting caught up with troublemakers. The police

1   said that Elroy was some kind of dope dealer. He has nothing to do with drugs. I guess the
2   District Attorney thought so too, because she let Elroy go. Elroy told me the DA dropped the
3   charges after he agreed to tell a judge about what happened. He was lucky because they
4   convicted a couple of those other boys. They went to prison. The DA told Elroy the next time
5   he got caught, he was going to jail. That put the fear of God in him. Of course, I told Elroy that
6   if he got in trouble again he would answer to me. I think that scared him even more. I got him
7   to volunteer with a lady at the University to do his wall art. He really does want to do the right
8   thing and is very sorry he got me into this mess.
9
10   It was about the middle of Month-8 when the Nita City Fire Department held a community
11   education meeting about sprinkler systems. I went to that meeting because I think we don't
12   do enough about fire prevention and safety. Lives could be saved if landlords would only
13   spend some money. The speakers told the group about how a sprinkler system could save
14   lives and protect property. After that meeting I knew that if Nita Gardens would install a
15   sprinkler system, it would make everyone in the building safer. The day after that meeting
16   I went down and talked with Ms. Longly about the building installing a fire sprinkler system.
17   She listened to what I had to say and then was very condescending.
18
19   She told me the building was safe enough and didn't need sprinklers. She said it would
20   cost millions to put a system in Nita Gardens and there was no money to pay for the costs.
21   When I told her she thought more about money than people she got mad and asked me to
22   leave. I couldn't believe she treated me that way. She just dismissed me as some crazy old
23   lady. I won't put up with that kind of treatment from anyone.
24
25   I took things into my own hands. I called all my friends in the building and told them about
26   how the city cared more about making rent money than our safety. I had Elroy get some
27   information on the school's computers. I showed people those papers and told them about
28   how Ms. Longly had blown me off and said the building was not worth upgrading. Everyone
29   was really upset when they heard my story. In Month-7some of my friends went with me
30   to ask Ms. Longly a second time. She tells us all the same thing—no sprinkler system. Some
31   of us decided that if the building wouldn't help us, we would force them to make a change.
32   I took a collection and had Elroy make up handbills and signs about sprinkler systems and
33   the management's position. Elroy did a great job and put our names on the bottom of the
34   posters. We put the handbills all over the building so folks would know about things. That
35   poster really stirred things up. A lot of people were plenty mad.
36
37   Then I organized some protests for the first floor. On Month-7, 13, YR-0 we had about 200
38   people who stood in the lobby and chanted. We did that a second time on Month-7, 20, and
39   then the building security cops came and told us we couldn't stay. The building still hasn't
40   done anything about the sprinklers. I guess it will never get done now.
41
42   Before the stuff about the sprinkler system I got along fine with Rachel Longly. She was nice
43   to me and my kids. After we flexed our muscles she wasn't so nice. She stopped saying "hi"
44   to us in the halls.

1 I was watching my Ps and Qs, but it was too late. I came home from work one afternoon to
2 find this paper stuffed under our door. It says because Elroy had been arrested for drugs and
3 he was part of some gang, we had to move out. It's really unfair. The DA dropped the charges
4 against Elroy. He's not guilty, and besides, all the troubles didn't even happen in the building.
5 They claim Elroy is in a street gang.
6
7 He spends some time with those boys playing basketball, but he has lots of friends. His best
8 friends are not part of that group. I'm sure this is some retaliatory BS because of what Elroy
9 and I did to let people know the building needs better fire protection. I know my rights. I'm
10 not stupid. I know they filed the papers four months after my protests. My lease says I can
11 join any tenant group I please. I have the right to protest building policies and inaction. They
12 aren't going to push me out. I'm here to stay. I can't afford to move somewhere else and keep
13 my babies with me. This just isn't fair!

Ladonna Johnson

Ladonna Johnson
Month-4, YR-0

STATEMENT OF ELROY JOHNSON

1   My name is Elroy Johnson. I'm sixteen years old and live with my grandmother, Ladonna Johnson,
2   in the Nita Gardens apartments. I've lived with my Gram since she moved here five years ago.
3   My sister and her baby also live with us. I go to the Nita City vocational high school.
4
5   My Gram is something. She's sixty-six and crippled up, but she works hard to make a home for
6   my sister and me. My mom died five years ago. She was a drunk and an addict and couldn't
7   really raise us. Gram stepped in and gave us a place to stay. She wants the best for us. Even
8   though she gets on my case all the time, I know she loves me and does what's best. Everyone
9   in the building likes Gram. She's always doing something for people—making cookies or
10 babysitting. I think everyone calls her Gram, and she likes it that way.
11
12 I'm an OK student at school, but my grades aren't great. Gram makes sure I do my homework
13 and get ready for tests. She's kind of a pain, but I know if it weren't for her I'd have dropped
14 out years ago.
15
16 She keeps telling me that if I stay in school, I'll make something of myself. I guess she's right. I'm
17 in the auto shop program at school, and when I graduate I'll be able to get a job as a mechanic.
18 What I would really like to do is be an artist, but I know there isn't any money in art. There is
19 this professor at Nita University who is helping me now. She tells me Urban Art is the hottest
20 new form of artwork. She has me helping her paint murals on buildings. Maybe that will help
21 me find a good job if we get evicted. I tell Gram that I want to be in the NBA, but I know I'm
22 no star. Gram thinks I want to be a pro. I'm not good enough, but it's fun to think I'll make it.
23 It'd be great if I could go to college on scholarship and get signed to the NBA. If I was a player,
24 I'd buy Gram her own house. Gram would kick my butt if I dropped out of school. Besides
25 basketball, mechanics, and art, I really like to skateboard. I ride all of the time. Mr. Comstocke
26 yells at me when I ride inside. I like to grind on some of the stair rails outside the building.
27
28 I spend a lot of time with friends from school and guys in the neighborhood. Many of the guys
29 I play street ball with are members of the Vice Lords, the local gang. There is a lot of pressure
30 on the street to join the Vice Lords, but I'm not really a member. None of my best friends are
31 in the gang, but some of the guys I play hoops with are members. Before the arrests, we hung
32 out together after school and on weekends. Some nights I would go down and find them and
33 shoot some hoops or mess around. Sometimes I would invite some of the Vice Lords to come
34 over and play ball. I never thought they would do more than play basketball.
35
36 My best friends are from school, not the street. Their names are Michelle Burgess, Tiffany
37 Fredericks, Angel Lopez, Walter Geoff, and Eddie Franklin. We call ourselves different names.
38 Michelle is Ampersand, Tiffany is Factor, Angel is Sky, Walt is Chill, Eddie is Brush, and they
39 call me Dr. Draw or Doc. We are a crew, and our name is Modern Neighborhood Art or MNA.
40 We are taggers and not a street gang. There is a big difference. We don't do hard drugs, and
41 our street art is about important social causes, like clean air and anti-war. We do our art on
42 buildings, dumpsters, and public transportation.

1   Some people call our work vandalism, but we know it is Urban Art. I can show you our log
2   book about the places we tagged. We are starting to build a pretty big rep among taggers. Our
3   specialty is "tagging the heavens," or things like overpasses and billboards. We are the first
4   team to paint the new overpass at I-34 and Ralston Road. We also did the roof on the new
5   Priceco store. We don't do residences. We design a statement in our sketch books and then
6   try it out on a place where I know they will paint over our practice work. I know Mr. Comstocke
7   paints over any graffiti right away. He never leaves graffiti up more than twelve hours. We
8   could never get any recognition from tagging at Nita Gardens, so we don't bother tagging
9   there. Now I hope I'll get recognition from working with Professor Stockbridge and that group
10   the police started to do murals.
11
12   I don't do hard drugs. Some of my friends do. I've only smoked some weed. I know I would
13   break Gram's heart if I did drugs, and I don't want to end up like my mom. In Month-10 I got
14   myself in trouble with the police. I was hanging outside with some of the guys from the
15   Vice Lords. We had just finished playing some hoops. The next thing I knew there were cops
16   everywhere with their guns out. I was scared. The cops arrested all of us for the sale and
17   possession of crack cocaine. Two of the guys were regular users and were dealing. They took
18   us all down to the police station. They charged everyone with either possession, possession
19   with intent to deal, or conspiracy. I was charged with conspiracy.
20
21   Gram let me sit in jail overnight as a lesson. The next day she bailed me out. I met with the
22   District Attorney. She tried hard to scare me and succeeded. She let me sweat for some time
23   and then came back and offered me a deal if I testified against the others. She made it sound
24   like I would do some serious jail time if I didn't cooperate. The public defender told me it
25   would be a good deal if I agreed.
26
27   I accepted the offer and agreed to testify if the charges were dismissed. I had to appear in
28   some kind of closed hearing. My lawyer told me it was the grand jury. I told them what I told
29   the DA. It turned out I didn't have to go to regular court because the others also agreed to
30   plea bargains. I was really relieved. Just the same, I got my dose of punishment from Gram.
31   From now on I'm staying away from anybody who's into drugs. I'm not really welcome around
32   the Vice Lords anyway. Frankly, I'm pretty scared they will do something to me. I don't think
33   they know I was going to testify against them. If they did, I think my life would be in danger.
34
35   Ms. Longly says the stuff I did threatened health, safety, and right to peacefully enjoy the
36   building. I don't know what she means. I don't think she's right. All I ever did was invite some
37   guys to play basketball and to spend time with them hanging out in the parking lot. No one
38   ever bothered other people from the building. Even the tagging didn't affect anyone except
39   Mr. Comstock and the building painters. Those guys would only stand around if it wasn't for
40   us making them do some work.
41
42   I didn't know it at the time, but my trouble turned into my Gram's trouble. Because of me, we
43   are getting evicted from our apartment. I don't think it's fair. I really didn't do anything wrong
44   except for hang with the wrong people. The DA dismissed the charges! This is BS! I know the
45   rules of the building.

1   My mother's death really had an impact on Gram. She's pretty paranoid about fire since my
2   mother was killed. She keeps our apartment spotless and makes us throw out any excess
3   paper and keep everything spotless. She makes the maintenance men clean up the laundry
4   and trash rooms. If there is a jam in the trash shoot, she calls and makes them clear it right
5   away. She reads everything she can about fire prevention. In Month-8, Gram went to this
6   presentation at the fire department. She came back all excited about sprinkler systems. She
7   told me that if they installed a sprinkler system in the Den it would save a whole bunch of lives
8   and property if there was ever a fire.
9
10 The next day she went down and had a visit with Ms. Longly, the building manager. She came
11 back really angry and upset, saying that Ms. Longly was only concerned about money and
12 acting like a big shot.
13
14 When my Gram gets mad you better put your head down and get out of the way. She has
15 some powerful anger. Gram called all her friends and the people whose kids she watches
16 and told them all about her conversation with Ms. Longly. Gram asked me if I would do some
17 computer research for her about sprinkler systems. I brought her some things from the Nita
18 Fire Department and the National Fire Protection Association. Then she had me make up
19 some flyers. I got the rest of the crew to help with those and some big signs. We really did
20 a great job, so I put my name on the bottom of the posters. She used the extra household
21 money and donations to get things printed. My Gram took part in the marches for civil rights.
22 She is big on public protest if she don't get her way. Right away she started this "Tenant Action
23 Committee." Gram got lots of people together, and we protested about the sprinkler system
24 in the lobby in Month-7. It was really cool. The second time we did it, on Month-7, 20, security
25 came and made us leave. Unfortunately, the protests did nothing to change things. Nothing
26 has happened to install sprinklers, and most of the people in the building have lost interest.
27
28 I know that Ms. Longly was really pissed off at Gram about the sprinkler protests. She stopped
29 me in the lobby one afternoon in Month-6 and asked me if I had anything to do with the
30 posters. I told her I made them up, and she could see my name on them. She told me that
31 what I did wasn't right. If I really knew what the building staff did to prevent fires, I wouldn't
32 be part of any protest. I told her I thought my Gram was right. Ms. Longly told me to be careful
33 because some things can come back and bite you. I didn't know what she meant then, but I
34 do now. I know she is using my bad luck to get back at Gram and me for the protests. I don't
35 think that's fair.
36
37 I'm really worried what will happen now. Gram can't afford to rent a place that's big enough
38 for all four of us. If this doesn't get fixed, I may have to drop out of school and get a job so
39 I can help Gram pay the new rent. It sucks! I'm trying to help by volunteering with Professor
40 Stockbridge and I plan to join that group Lieutenant Wherder started.

Elroy Johnson

Elroy Johnson
Month-4, YR-0

STATEMENT OF ANNE WORTHINGTON STOCKBRIDGE

1   My name is Anne Worthington Stockbridge. I am a Professor of Art History and Urban Art
2   Studies at the University of Nita. I am also the director of the department. I have been with
3   the University of Nita since YR-21, moving up the educational ranks from assistant professor
4   to full professor over these twenty-one years. In addition to directing the School of Art and Art
5   History, I teach a full load of classes at the university and maintain a high level of scholarship.
6   My concentration is divided between Urban Art and its history and French Art as it appears
7   in the United States. I have been asked to offer my opinion on whether the work of a group
8   known as Modern Neighborhood Art should be considered Urban Art or gang-related graffiti.
9   I have also been asked to comment on whether Urban Art would have the negative effect
10 of threatening the health, safety, or right to peaceful enjoyment of the residents of the Nita
11 Gardens public housing facility.
12
13 I agreed to testify as an expert witness for Ladonna Johnson without charging a fee after
14 reading about her protests and the eviction case against her on the Internet. I am familiar
15 with the artwork of her grandson, Elroy Johnson, as part of my research on Urban Art in
16 Nita City. I was offended by the City Housing Authority's treatment of Mrs. Johnson and the
17 assertion that Elroy Johnson's artwork was considered criminal gang behavior.
18
19 Urban Art, sometimes known as "graffiti," is a style of art that relates to cities and city life. It is
20 often created by artists who live in or have a passion for city life. The term urban means "from
21 the city." Sometimes Urban Art is called "street art." The style of this art is mostly cartoon
22 based, but it is sometimes realistic. The art may sometimes be viewed as vandalism and
23 destruction of property. Most recently, however, critics and those who appreciate modern
24 forms of artistic expression view Urban Art as a new form of public art. Urban artists often use
25 their work as a forum for political expression or to beautify more decrepit areas of their city.
26
27 The debate about Urban Art began with the tagging of subway cars in New York City and
28 spread throughout the United States in the early 1970s. It is hard for residents of Nita City to
29 conceptualize what the subways of New York were like more than twenty years ago. I remind
30 my students of this fact when we discuss the origins of Urban Art. I use the court decision
31 in the criminal case *People v. Goetz* to illustrate my point. That seminal case, as students of
32 New York history know, involved the vigilantism of Bernard Goetz on a subway car in 1984.
33
34 Without touching on the moral or legal issues raised by the case, the students review
35 comments by people who had grown up in New York and people who had not. Those who
36 had not been raised in the city had a difficult time understanding what the subways were like
37 in the 1980s. You may have difficulty imagining how concerned New Yorkers were about their
38 graffiti-covered, mechanically unsound, crime-ridden trains. In those days there was real fear
39 about safety, and graffiti was a contributing factor.
40
41 In the same year as the Goetz shooting, Martha Cooper and Henry Chalfant released a
42 book called *Subway Art*. The tome—a picture book—was one of the first to focus on the

1   graffiti-covered subways as an art form. Today, Urban Art is not a reflection on the lawlessness
2   of the city, but rather a means of expression for young artists from disadvantaged backgrounds.
3   Thanks to a variety of factors, the subway system in New York City is no longer as dangerous.
4   These days, we have no qualms about riding the Nita City subway at 2:00 a.m. Thanks to
5   the excellent job done by the Nita City police, people just do not worry about their safety in
6   public places in the same ways as 1980s New York City. People's perceptions about graffiti
7   are substantially different in YR-0 than they were in those times. Graffiti does not prompt
8   the same feelings of unrest and terror. In fact, most view graffiti with a level of interest in the
9   same way they look at other modern art forms.
10
11 Urban Artists are also known as "taggers" or "writers." Even though many classify their
12 behavior as criminal, there is a significant difference between tagging crews and actual
13 criminal or street gangs. Tagging crews are motivated to write graffiti for the sake of art,
14 not for actual criminal purposes. Members of tagging crews may not even be from the
15 inner city. In Nita City, as well as other locations, taggers may come from middle and upper
16 income homes in addition to those from less privileged backgrounds. For taggers, graffiti is
17 a source of entertainment and political statement that comes from decorating public and
18 private property. Taggers often have risk-taking personalities. Many taggers also participate in
19 high-risk activities such as those found in extreme sports—skateboarding and in-line skating,
20 BMX bicycling, snow boarding, and skiing. One of the newer activities of taggers is freestyle
21 walking, where the walker uses leaps and air moves, clever footwork, dance, or any non-
22 traditional walking movement to move around the city. Some taggers may associate with
23 street gangs as another means of risk taking. They are usually not street gang members and
24 can be referred to as a gang "wannabe." Street gangs sometimes hire taggers to advertise on
25 the gang's behalf. In some states, taggers carry weapons to defend themselves from members
26 of street gangs. However, taggers are usually not violent.
27
28 Taggers join together in groups called crews. The typical crew has between three and ten
29 members. A crew is often co-ed, with males and females working side by side. Sometimes
30 crews put up pieces by working together—with one creating the outline of the design and
31 others filling in the colors. Each member then signs his or her name to the completed piece,
32 which is short for "masterpiece." Taggers are often highly intelligent and have ironic senses of
33 humor. Many will take on causes, such as "save the environment" or "free political prisoners."
34
35 Tagger graffiti is easily recognized and substantially different from street-gang graffiti. Tagger
36 graffiti is more stylized and artistic—with fat, wild, or geometric letters. It usually contains
37 brighter colors and has more details. Tagger graffiti may also incorporate pictures. In addition
38 to spray paint, taggers make use of very wide markers, name tags or other stickers, paint
39 sticks, and sharp objects, which are used to etch glass. Gang-based writing has none of these
40 stylized attributes and is far more primitive. Most urban artists view gang graffiti with disdain
41 and do not want to be associated with this un-artistic form of communication.
42
43 Tagger crews earn recognition through the number of tags they make, the size or area covered
44 by the tag, and the degree of challenge in placing the tag. Tagger crews are unlike street gangs
45 in that they are not usually territorial and will attempt to display their work wherever they

1   can find a clean wall. Favorite places for tags are freeways, trains, and subways, and places
2   that have never been hit by graffiti. However, tags are never put on street surfaces. The goal
3   is to break new ground. Taggers get a rush from tagging in an unusual location like a rooftop
4   or overpass.
5
6   Tagging is often a way of life and a culture unto itself. Many taggers believe they are creating a
7   form of artwork that they refer to as "aerosol art." There is often competition between tagging
8   crews to determine who the best artist is. Carrying sketch books, talking about tagging, and
9   recording projects through photographs or video are a big part of tagger culture. The Internet
10   provides a vast source of comparative ideas and a place for friends to view new hits. Part
11   of my work with taggers is to make this art form more accessible to other members of the
12   community.
13
14   Urban Artists follow a strict set of unwritten rules. To summarize those rules: First, Urban Art,
15   or graffiti, is not done on the car of a civilian—a person who is not an Urban Artist. Second, it
16   is acceptable to write, or put art, on the car of another Urban Artist if you have an issue with
17   that person. Third, Urban Art is not to be done on the ground, meaning artists should not use
18   the street or pavement as a canvas. Fourth, Urban Art should not be placed on the private
19   property of a civilian. It is acceptable to tag, or paint, on another Urban Artist's house if you
20   have an issue with that person. Virtually all Urban Artists are aware of these rules and strictly
21   follow them. Failure to "obey" these rules means shunning by the community of artists.
22
23   I am familiar with the works of the tagging crew Modern Neighborhood Art or MNA. While
24   they are not known on a national level with the likes of Shepard Fairey, Above, Akayism, Akay
25   and Adams, Banks, Adam Neate, Mark Jenkins, Dubelyoo, or Jorge Rodriguez-Gerada, they are
26   considered one of the up-and-coming groups of Urban Artists in Nita City. They have grown
27   from a local presence to city-wide notoriety. As Urban Artists, these kids are very good. They
28   have a sharp sense of humor and great style. Their big projects make some blighted areas
29   look far better. I could never imagine how anyone would find the MNA's art to be threatening
30   or suggesting violence. Their images are political in nature and often satirical.
31
32   I met with Elroy Johnson on several occasions, both for my work on this case and earlier for
33   other research and current academic projects. During my non-case-related research I learned
34   that Elroy is considered by many in the art community as a rising Urban Art star. It is rumored
35   he is the leader of MNA. I spent some time interviewing Elroy Johnson about the graffiti in
36   Nita City. He is passionate about the subject of Urban Art. He shared his sketch book with me
37   and is quite proud of his work. I told him I recognized some his work from around the city,
38   and we discussed using photographs of these works as part of a show I was developing for
39   the University's gallery.
40
41   As part of my research for this case I walked the neighborhood around Nita Gardens on two
42   occasions. The first time I walked the area by myself, and the second time Elroy Johnson
43   accompanied me. I used the opportunities to look specifically at both the gang graffiti that
44   was currently present and other pieces of Urban Art. In both instances there was not much
45   gang graffiti present. The Nita City police have done a good job educating the public about the

1 dangers of gang graffiti, and most businesses and residences remove the gang graffiti almost
2 immediately. The Urban Art was more prevalent, as many now view it not as graffiti, but as
3 art. The examples of gang graffiti I did view demonstrated a lack of artistic touch. There were
4 a great deal of symbols plus names and numbers. It was clear these were designed to mark
5 territory and make threats. Every example could be traced to the Vice Lords gang. These can
6 be seen in the two photographs in Exhibit 9. The Urban Art was easily distinguished by its use
7 of color, stylized writing, figures and other images, three-dimensional imagery, etc. The sharp
8 contrasts can be seen in the photographs in Exhibit 10. As you look at the photographs you
9 can see how someone might be intimidated by the scrawlings of the gang graffiti. The Urban
10 Art by comparison shows no hostility and even complements the buildings where it has been
11 painted.
12
13 On my second visit to the neighborhood, I walked with Elroy Johnson. We discussed the
14 differences between gang graffiti and tagger graffiti. I asked Elroy to give me a running
15 commentary on the various pieces of graffiti we saw as we took our tour. I pressed him about
16 the gang graffiti in the neighborhood around Nita Gardens. I asked him about these tags,
17 but he claimed to have no knowledge about who was involved and was quite scornful about
18 the quality. It was clear Elroy had no part in the criminal use of graffiti as expressed by these
19 amateur gang symbols and messages. I admit that someone as talented as Elroy Johnson
20 could easily have adopted this style and created what I saw. However, Elroy's comments to
21 me seemed genuine, and his disdain for the gang graffiti was clear.
22
23 During my second visit to this neighborhood I also took the opportunity to speak with several
24 people I met during my tour of the neighborhood. I specifically asked them how they felt
25 about both the graffiti and Urban Art in the area. I showed photographs of examples of both
26 gang graffiti and Urban Art. Every person I spoke with saw the distinction between the gang
27 writing and the Urban Art. Some of those I spoke with indicated they were disturbed by both
28 types of examples. Others told me they liked the Urban Art and felt it improved the feel of
29 the neighborhood. On each occasion, I asked if the person felt threatened or unsafe when
30 they saw these writings. The answers often depended on the age of the person I questioned.
31 The older people more often indicated a fear of these writings and those who created them.
32 Some told me they felt any writing was an invasion of their personal space. Others were more
33 positive toward the Urban Art. Those people indicated the Urban Art examples made the
34 neighborhood look better and were a way of cleaning up the area. As opposed to the few who
35 indicated fear, these interviewees thought the Urban Art created a sense of neighborhood
36 pride and a desire to improve the area. All together, I spoke with approximately fifteen people.
37 Each conversation lasted between two and ten minutes. Six of the people I interviewed were
38 residents of Nita Gardens. Their opinions were split evenly between liking Urban Art and
39 disliking gang graffiti.
40
41 Mr. Johnson is currently helping me with a project that recreates famous graffiti pieces from
42 1980s New York City. All of the works are reinterpretations of that art, altering what might be
43 perceived as violent or antagonistic information into a more neutral and palatable message
44 to the general public.

1   Graffiti or Urban Art is prohibited by a city ordinance in Nita City. I must say I personally
2   strongly disagree with this law. There will come a day when the city's leadership recognizes
3   the value of Urban Art and repeals this silly law.
4
5   It is my expert opinion that the Urban Artwork of Elroy Johnson and MNA is not threatening or
6   suggestive of violence in any way. I consider it a prime example of the best of Urban Art being
7   done in Nita City. It certainly rivals much of the best work you find in other cities. Calling these
8   wonderful pieces of art criminal is similar to calling political cartoons and posters illegal. Such
9   statements of protest have been used for centuries as a means of expression. As a class of
10   artwork they are beyond value. Only people with no appreciation of art would ever consider
11   the Urban Art murals done by MNA and Elroy Johnson threatening or calling for violence.
12   People fear change, and Urban Art is all about change. You could make the analogy that
13   "hip-hop" music advocates violence and is threatening. The reality is these new forms reflect
14   change in society, not a call for anarchy. There is absolutely no reason why people should be
15   put in fear by seeing Urban Art.
16
17   I recently read the online article in *Your Hub* about the latest peace mural in Nita City. If
18   the Gang Task Force holds out that Elroy Johnson is a hero for his artwork, I cannot believe
19   they would also accuse him of criminal activity and use his natural creativity as a reason for
20   eviction.
21
22   I really have no knowledge of the arrest of Elroy Johnson as part of a drug case. I can only
23   say from having interviewed him that I cannot believe he would be involved in drugs or gang
24   activity. He is not a violent person.
25
26   I would like to see Elroy Johnson enrolled in art school. I believe he has the talent to become
27   a professional artist.

Anne Worthington Stockbridge

Anne Worthington Stockbridge
Month-1, YR-0

STATEMENT OF DETECTIVE ROBERTA BEHMER

1   My name is Roberta Behmer. I am a detective with the Nita City Policy Department, currently
2   assigned to the Gang Task Force. I have been employed as a peace officer for the past
3   ten years. I joined the Nita City Police shortly after I graduated from Nita Lakes Community
4   College in YR-10. I attended the police academy and was hired by the department that same
5   year. I initially was assigned as a street officer and did beat patrol. I worked in two districts
6   for the first eight years of my career. I passed the sergeant's examination in my seventh year
7   and was promoted to that rank in YR-8. Shortly thereafter I joined the Gang Task Force. In the
8   past year I received my Detective's shield from the department. The majority of my work with
9   the Gang Task Force is enforcing the drug laws of the State of Nita. I am also the liaison with
10   the United States Drug Enforcement Administration (DEA) and the United States Attorney's
11   office for Nita.
12
13   My current work with the Gang Task Force is to coordinate and lead large scale enforcement
14   operations that require coordination with the rest of the department and the federal
15   government.
16
17   I was the officer in charge of the operation of Month-10, 8, where we arrested a number of
18   minors and adults for the possession and sale of crack cocaine. The arrests were based on
19   reports from residents of Nita Gardens and others in the area around that complex. These
20   reports placed gang members either on the premises of Nita Gardens or in the parking lot
21   of the complex for the purpose of selling illegal drugs. The arrests were part of an ongoing
22   investigation targeting the Vice Lords as one of the largest distributors of cocaine in Nita City.
23   That campaign continues today. We have been successful in many of our efforts as our
24   investigations have culminated in a series of arrests and convictions throughout Nita City. The
25   arrests at Nita Gardens were targeted for Month-10, 8, YR-1. Twenty arrests were made in that
26   operation. I consider this campaign very successful as we were able to get five convictions. It
27   put a serious dent in the Vice Lords's drug operations for a number of months.
28
29   As the officer in charge, I was personally involved with the arrests at Nita Gardens on Month-10.
30   My responsibilities included working with the rest of the department to secure a sufficient
31   number of officers to successfully conduct the operation and to arrange for unmarked and
32   marked vehicles to transport personnel and those arrested. I also informed the DEA and
33   U.S. Attorney's office about the operation and invited them to participate in the arrests.
34
35   On the day in question we set up a command post down the street from Nita Gardens. From
36   there I was able to observe the parking lot. I was in radio communication with all units.
37   At approximately 5:00 p.m., units were deployed to the location at 874 Jackson Avenue and
38   surrounding area. These included two unmarked vans, two marked cruisers, and a command
39   unit. The confidential informant was with us and was equipped with a radio transmitter.
40
41   At 7:05 p.m., a group of approximately twenty people left the main entrance of Nita Gardens
42   and moved to the parking lot. There were both men and women in the group. They appeared

1 to be aged from fourteen to twenty-one years old. From my vantage point it appeared the
2 group was engaged in conversation. It was a party-like atmosphere.
3
4 At 7:20 p.m. I sent the informant to meet with the people he had indicated were to sell him
5 drugs.
6
7 At approximately 7:30 what appeared to be a transaction occurred between the informant and
8 a member of the group, who we later identified as Jerry Collins. I ordered officers to surround
9 the group and apprehend the perpetrators. Four police vehicles proceeded into parking lot.
10
11 Officers found drugs and paraphernalia on people in the group. After conferring with my
12 federal colleagues I decided to arrest all of those who were in the group. I arranged for bus
13 transportation, and all were transported to the 12th Precinct station.
14
15 On arrival at the 12th Precinct station, Detectives Wasilewski and Taggert and I began
16 processing prisoners. The decision was made to charge each prisoner with one or all of the
17 following drug-related offenses: possession of a controlled substance, possession with intent
18 to sell a controlled substance, or conspiracy to sell a controlled substance. Elroy Johnson was
19 charged with conspiracy to sell a controlled substance.
20
21 On Month-10, 11, District Attorney Michael Burton and I met with Elroy Johnson at around
22 2:00 p.m. DA Burton informed Johnson of his rights and told him the charges against him.
23 At that time Johnson waived his right to counsel and agreed to speak with us. It was clear
24 Johnson was a very scared young man. He agreed to cooperate in return for his charges being
25 dismissed. The agreement was straight forward. In return for testifying against members of
26 the Vice Lords, the City would dismiss any charges against Johnson. This proved to be a very
27 positive agreement for the government as the charges against Johnson were quite weak and
28 there was little chance of a conviction.
29
30 Johnson later testified at a grand jury hearing, giving testimony against Jerry Collins and
31 Albert Decalbe. His testimony was instrumental in the grand jury indictments against those
32 two individuals. As a result of the indictments, both individuals pleaded guilty and are now
33 serving in the Nita state prison. Johnson's name was never released, and he did not have to
34 testify. As we agreed, charges against him were dismissed.

Roberta Behmer

Roberta Behmer
Month-3, YR-0

UNIVERSITY OF NITA

ANNE WORTHINGTON STOCKBRIDGE
SCHOOL OF ART AND ART HISTORY
PROFESSOR OF ART HISTORY AND URBAN STUDIES
SISK ART BUILDING, ROOM 132
2121 LAMONT STREET
NITA CITY, NITA

Month-1, 25, YR-0

Nelson Ridgeway, Esq.
Nita Legal Services
1875 Larimer Street, Suite 200
Nita City, Nita

RE: Does graffiti affect the health, safety, or right to peaceful enjoyment of the residents of
                Nita Gardens

CLIENT: Ladonna Johnson

Dear Mr. Ridgeway:

At your request I have done an analysis and comparison of graffiti and Urban Art in the area surrounding Nita Gardens Housing Development. You asked for my opinion on whether the work of a group known as Modern Neighborhood Art should be considered Urban Art or gang-related graffiti. You also asked for my opinion on whether such art would have a detrimental effect on the health, safety, or right to peaceful enjoyment of the residents of that building.

I performed the following activities in forming my opinions on both these questions:

1. Reviewed photographs of graffiti and Urban Art from various parts of Nita City, including the immediate neighborhood where Nita Gardens is located;

2. Personally toured the area surrounding Nita Gardens to view graffiti and Urban Art on two occasions;

3. Interviewed Elroy Johnson about his work as an Urban Artist;

4. Interviewed residents of the areas regarding their feeling about graffiti and Urban Art; and

5. Reviewed current literature regarding Urban Art and its affect on society.

The review of photographs was based on pictures taken from April YR-2 through August YR-1. The photographs were taken by a variety of professional photographers, police photographers, and students from my classes at the University. Images were recorded from a wide variety of locations throughout Nita City, including the area surrounding Nita Gardens. I reviewed a total of 300 photographs, which included examples of gang graffiti and Urban Art.

More recently, I made two tours of the neighborhood approximately seven days apart. The first tour was taken on a weekday morning and covered a ten-square-block area surrounding Nita Gardens. It was a thorough review of all streets, alleys, public places, and business sites. During this tour I observed approximately twenty different examples of gang graffiti and Urban Art. The second tour occurred six days later. The tour occurred on a weekend afternoon. I was accompanied for a portion of that time by Elroy Johnson, grandson of your client, Ladonna Johnson. Mr. Johnson is a self-described Urban Artist of some note. I asked Mr. Johnson to accompany me in an effort to review other pieces of graffiti and Urban Art and specifically identify Urban Art created by Mr. Johnson and the tagger crew know as Modern Neighborhood Art. Mr. Johnson identified three large murals and five other examples of his group's work. After I left Mr. Johnson, I used the tour to interview a number of residents of the area about their feelings about both gang graffiti and Urban Art.

My review of current literature regarding the impact of Urban Art on society shows two very different views. The more conservative view is that Urban Art is vandalism, a trespass on private property, and a defacing of public property. This view is widely held by the law enforcement community and some legislators. Others feel less strongly about the negative impact of Urban Art, suggesting it is a new form of public expression, an outlet of artistic expression for young artists who have no other forum, a means of demonstrating neighborhood pride and political expression, and a process for reclaiming areas from urban blight. Included in my research were the following:

One Place After Another, Miwon Kwon. MIT Press, 2003.

Public Art by the Book, edited by Barbara Goldstein. 2005.

Dialogues in Public Art, edited by Tom Finkelpearl. MIT Press, 2000.

The Interventionists: Users' Manual for the Creative Disruption of Everyday Life, edited by Nato Thompson and Gregory Sholette. MASS MoCA, 2004.

Conversation Pieces: Community + Communication in Modern Art, Grant Kester. University of California Press, 2004.

Mapping the Terrain: New Genre Public Art, edited by Suzanne Lacy. Bay Press, 1995.

Evictions: Art and Spatial Politics, Rosalyn Deutsche. MIT Press, 1998.

In/Different Spaces: Place and Memory in Visual Culture, Victor Burgin. University of California Press, 1996.

Art, Space and the City: Public Art and Urban Futures, Malcolm Miles. 1997.

Spirit Poles and Flying Pigs: Public Art and Cultural Democracy in American Communities, Erika Lee Doss. 1995

Critical Issues in Public Art: Content, Context, and Controversy, Harriet Senie and Sally Webster. 1993

Cement or Canvas: Aerosol Art & The Changing Face of Graffiti in the 21st Century, Bradley J. Bartolomeo. Anthropology Honors Thesis, 2001.

I believe it is important to make a connection between "Public Art" and "Urban Art." Monuments, memorials, and civic statuary are perhaps the oldest and most obvious form of officially sanctioned public art, although it could be said that architectural sculpture and even architecture itself is more widespread and fulfills the definition of public art. Increasingly, most aspects of the built environment are seen as legitimate candidates for consideration as, or location for, public art, including street furniture, lighting, and graffiti.

Some artists working in this discipline use the freedom afforded by an outdoor site to create very large works that would be unfeasible in a gallery. Among the works of the last thirty years that have met the greatest positive and negative, critical and popular acclaim are pieces by Christo, Robert Smithson, Andy Goldsworthy, and Anthony Gormley, where the artwork reacts to or incorporates its environment. For artists working in low income neighborhoods it is often difficult to receive permission to create their art. For many, frustration with the system and an inability to find places to produce their works leads to conflict with local laws and a failure to get, or even seek, permission to create.

Artists making public art range from the greatest masters such as Michelangelo, Pablo Picasso, and Joan Miró, to those who specialize in public art such as Claes Oldenburg and Pierre Granche, to anonymous artists who make surreptitious interventions. This last group often includes inner city artist and has led to the creation of the term "Urban Art."

If the art and literature of a particular culture are often examined for insights into the preoccupations of the best minds of that society, should not graffiti be given the same consideration? Does a drawing have to be plastered on a page to qualify for such analysis? Do we stop searching for the inner meaning of a painting or a poem when it appears on a wall merely because we do not happen to acknowledge the wall as a suitable receptacle for art or literature?

Do we stop trying to understand what motivated the artist or the writer merely because he chose to express his thoughts through some unconventional medium? I suggest that graffiti carries the same weight as other forms of public art.

The word graffiti comes from the Latin word "graffito," meaning "to write." Today, the term is used to denote any drawing, scribbling, or writing on a public surface. Though this kind of writing is not new, a graffiti culture emerged with the hip-hop scene late last century in New York City. Graffiti artists like Keith Haring and "Taki 183" drew media attention and spawned imitators known as "taggers," who use spray paint and other materials to mark private and public walls, including the outside of industrial facilities. Once mostly an inner-city, lower-income protest, tagging has branched out in the 21st century. For instance, Philadelphia police recently apprehended a twenty-seven-year-old stockbroker who drove to tagging sites in his BMW.

The common name for many forms of Urban Art is "graffiti." This may be a misnomer as graffiti often has negative connotations. Urban Art may also be referred to as "street art." Originally based on forms of writing, Urban Art has now evolved into a combination of writing, cartoon-based images, and, sometimes, political or social messages. Because "tagging" or Urban Art is done on public and private property it may sometimes be viewed as vandalism and destruction of property. This sense of criminal behavior is beginning to evolve into a view that Urban Art is a new form of public art. Urban artists often use their work as a forum for either political expression or to beautify more decrepit areas of their city.

Gang "graffiti" is very different from Urban Art. Gang graffito, the singular of graffiti, is often the first indication that street gangs are active in a community. Graffiti is the newspaper, the billboard, the Internet of the world of street gangs, and serves to mark the gang's power and status. Graffiti marks territorial boundaries and serves as a warning to other gangs that the area marked with unique signs and symbols is the territory or "turf" of a particular gang. Graffiti warns intruders or trespassers from rival gangs, and even policemen, that they are not welcome. It may also be an advertisement for the sale of drugs or a memorial to a fallen fellow gang member.

Tagger works are easily recognized and substantially different from street-gang graffiti. Tagger "graffiti" is more stylized and artistic—with fat, wild, or geometric letters. It usually contains brighter colors and has more details. Tagger graffiti may also incorporate pictures. In addition to spray paint, taggers make use of very wide markers, name tags or other stickers, paint sticks, and sharp objects that are used to etch glass. Gang-based writing has none of these stylized attributes and is far more primitive.

My conclusions are as follows:

1. The work of Elroy Johnson and Modern Neighborhood Art is not gang graffiti.

I've include with this report images of several projects claimed by Modern Neighborhood Art (MNA). Elroy Johnson also provided me with examples from his sketch book, and I have attached an example to this report. As noted above, gang-related graffiti uses signs and symbols to mark territory, warn or threaten other gangs, advertise criminal activities, or memorialize fallen members. It is primitive lettering, often drawn with markers. Comparing the MNA work, you can easily see these images are far more stylized and offer visual messages that differ from those presented by gangs. This work incorporates color and mixed media, uses pictures, and makes a statement. It is also clearly signed by the tagging crew. Elroy Johnson's work in particular also matches this style. You see similarities from Mr. Johnson's sketch book in the public presentations by MNA. There is no question of the distinction between the two—this is clearly not gang-related work.

2. Urban Art does not have a detrimental effect on the health, safety, or right to peaceful enjoyment of the residents of Nita Gardens.

The presence of gang graffiti can cause people to feel unsafe. It creates a perception that nobody cares about the area, and it may even encourage other more serious crimes. Negative gang graffiti impacts the health and wellbeing of a community. Public spaces that have writing may be avoided by legitimate users, and if the graffiti is racist or contains discriminatory themes, it can personally offend individuals or community groups. There is no question that gang-related graffiti can cause deep concerns among neighborhood residents. The area around Nita Gardens is clearly the territory of the Vice Lords street gang. I believe any discomfort felt by residents of Nita Gardens is caused by the mere presence of gang members in the area. As indicated above, "Urban Art" is a new form of "Public Art." New forms of artistic expression may be met with public derision and disapproval. This does not mean the works are not art or should be considered detrimental to the health, safety, or right to peaceful enjoyment of a property. In open societies, artists often find public art useful in promoting their ideas or establishing a censorship-free means of contact with viewers. The art may be intentionally ephemeral, as in the case of temporary installations and performance pieces. Such art has a spontaneous quality. It is characteristically displayed in urban environments without the consent of authorities. In time, however, some art of this kind achieves official recognition. Examples include situations in which the line between graffiti and "guerilla" public art is blurred, such as the art of John Fekner placed on billboards, the early works of Keith Haring (executed without permission in advertising poster holders in the New York City Subway) and the current work of Banksy. The Northern Irish murals and those in Los Angeles were often responses to periods of conflict. The art provided an effective means of communication both within and beyond a distressed group within the larger society. In the long run the work proved useful in establishing dialogue and helping to bridge the social rifts that fueled the original conflicts.

Graffiti, like any other art form, can be an aesthetic tool used to better understand the social, political, and cultural attitudes deeply embedded within a particular group. I am not necessarily claiming that art defines culture, but rather, I am asserting the notion that it is a visual representation of particular beliefs and attitudes, and quite certainly, it is a material manifestation that, by nature, has the ability to contribute to culture. All people, whether a member of the graffiti community or not, can see the art on the wall; the meaning is subject to interpretation, and thus the intended meaning and audience may be overlooked, transformed into an unintended statement.

Many of those I spoke with in my investigation were able to distinguish between gang-related graffiti and Urban Art. A majority of those interviewed had a positive feeling regarding Urban Art and expressed some appreciation for the artistic nature of both murals and smaller works. When shown examples of Urban Art, most people felt it was not a threat to their health, safety, or right to peaceful enjoyment. Most expressed feelings that these works helped to beautify the neighborhood. The argument that all residents of Nita Gardens feel their health, safety, or right to peaceful enjoyment are threatened is clearly an over-reaching by the building's administration. **Except for a few, limited examples, the residents of Nita Gardens are not concerned about the instances of Urban Art in the area. There is no rational belief that such artwork threatens anyone's health, safety, or right to peaceful enjoyment. To the contrary, I believe this art improves peoples feeling about their residence.**

As we agreed by telephone, I am donating my services in this matter. I believe strongly in the work of Elroy Johnson and support his family in retaining their lease.

Should you have questions or concerns about this report, please feel free to contact me.

Very truly yours,

Anne Worthington Stockbridge

Anne Worthington Stockbridge

Professor and Director

attachments

Examples of Urban Art in Area of Nita Gardens

Example 1 - located on Jackson Avenue (3 blocks from Nita Gardens)

Example 2 - located in alley at 1783 Pierce Street (8 blocks from Nita Gardens)

ANNE WORTHINGTON STOCKBRIDGE
SCHOOL OF ART AND ART HISTORY
PROFESSOR OF ART HISTORY AND URBAN STUDIES
SISK ART BUILDING, ROOM 132
2121 LAMONT STREET
NITA CITY, NITA

Education

BA, Art History, summa cum laude, Concordia College
MA, Art History, University of Wisconsin-Madison
MA, Urban Anthropology, University of Colorado at Denver
PhD, Art History, Boston University

Professional Experience

Director, School of Art and Art History, University of Nita, YR-12 to present
Professor, University of Nita, YR-14 to present, University of Nita
Associate Professor, University of Nita, YR-18 to YR-14
Assistant Professor, University of Nita, YR-19 to YR-18
Assistant Professor, University of Montana, YR-23 to YR-19
Mellon Faculty Fellow in the Humanities, Harvard University, YR-24 to YR-23
Assistant Professor, University of Maine, YR-25 to YR-24

Selected Publications

Urban Art and Politics—Expression of Opinion versus Destruction of Property in New Trends in Modern Art, ed. Joyce Goodspeed, 13–39. Atlantic World Series. (Nita University Press YR-2).
Graffiti as a Means of Constitutionally Protected Speech, 68 Mont. L. Rev. 375 (YR-4).
The New Urban Artist: Bringing Art to the Ghetto (Overlook Press, YR-6).
Russian Political Posters and Urban Art: The Use of Public Space to Affect Public Opinion, 25 The Art Journal 57 (Spring YR-6).
Transformative Triptychs in Multicultural America, American Art (Spring YR-10).
The Woodman of the World Monument Program, Markers XX 1–29 (YR-16).
American Political Posters of the Revolutionary War, New Hampshire Press (YR-20).
Women and Graffiti: Feminist Expression in Urban Art, 24 Journal of Women's Studies 75 (YR-22).
The French Dining Room in Turn of the Century America, Winterthur Portfolio, 37 (Winter YR-23).
French Mania: The Unknown Francophile Period in American Art and Culture (Treadstone Press, YR-24).
Going French: French Painting in America 1609–1990 (Frederick Press, YR-25).

Recent Exhibits

Fall YR-0	Subway Art: A reinterpretation of New York subway art. A series of urban murals created throughout Nita City by various local urban artists.
Spring YR-1	Urban Artists of Nita City YR-10 to YR-2 (A photograph retrospective), NUMA (Nita University Gallery of Modern Art)
April YR-5	Going French: French Art in America 1875–1900. (Nita Museum of Art)

Courses Taught
    Introduction to Contemporary Art
    Art History—The Middle Ages
    Art History—European Artists of the 20th Century
    Art History—The Use of Art as Political Expression
    Seminar in Political Expression and Free Speech
    Art Conservation

Presentations
Is Graffiti Public Art? Interview on Nita Public Radio, November 15, YR-3
Social Commentary or Gang Communication: Differences Between Urban Art and Gang Tagging, Symposium on Urban Anthropology. University of St. Claire, Toronto, Ontario, Canada, April 20, YR-4
The Popularity of French Pastoral Art in Early 20th Century America. Nita Art Museum Public Program, September 25, YR-5

Current Research Projects
Gender Politics in Urban Art
A study investigating the gendering of urban art. This book-in-progress reviews urban art by women from YR-20 through the present and the effects of gender on the men and women who use urban art as a means of expression.

Nita Cemeteries: Sculpture Gardens of the Dead
This book-in-progress considers pioneer community cemeteries and their arts throughout the state of Nita. Chapters include: From Boot Hill to Fair Haven—The Transformation of Nita Graveyards; Tombstone Carvers and Monument Makers of Nita; Marble Works and the Gendered Cemetery; Mail Order Monuments; Nita Cemeteries in a National Context; and The Sepulchral Garden in Nita Life.

Nita City Police Department
Gang Task Force
One Police Plaza
Nita City, Nita

Month-1, 15, YR-0

Susan Maranetty, Attorney
Nita City Housing Authority—Legal Department
875 Main Street, AHEF-14
Nita City, Nita

RE: Expert testimony regarding graffiti

Dear Attorney Maranetty:

I am responding to your request for the police department to provide your department with an expert witness regarding graffiti for a pending eviction matter. I was asked by the Chief of Police to respond to your request and provide whatever services you need.

I am the commanding officer of the department's Gang Task Force. In that role I supervise a team of officers as we enforce state and local laws with a specific emphasis on gang-related activities in Nita City. A part of our work relates to enforcing the city's ordinances on graffiti. We also spend a good deal of time reading and interpreting gang-related writing in the city.

I am qualified to assist you as an expert for the following reasons:

1. Education and training in criminology and anthropology;

2. Speaking and writing on gang-related graffiti on a national level;

3. Experience as a beat officer and member of the Gang Task Force;

4. Awards for meritorious citations for work in the inner city community;

5. Previous testimony as an expert witness on graffiti and gang activities.

You requested an opinion on whether graffiti creates an atmosphere that threatens the health, safety, or right to peaceful enjoyment of public housing premises. Specifically your request references the work of a tagger gang know as Modern Neighborhood Art, or MNA, and its leader, Elroy Johnson. I am prepared to offer an affirmative opinion on that question.

Jonathan Kellerman referred to graffiti as "the hieroglyphics of rage." (Kellerman, Jonathan, *Bad Love*, Bantam Books / Random House, 1994, p. 161.) Viewed in this light, those who write on public and private surfaces without permission are using this medium to express their rage at society. Throughout the United States, jurisdictions have labeled graffiti as vandalism. Here in Nita City, writing on any public or private surface without permission is a municipal offense. It is against the law, and the Nita City Police are charged with enforcing this law. Graffiti should not be tolerated in any community. It frequently leads to the degradation of a neighborhood and the devaluation of property. Studies have shown in many cases that if graffiti is not removed and is left unchecked, more and more graffiti will appear. The removal of graffiti is extremely costly, and it costs Nita City huge sums of money to reclaim and beautify neighborhoods or communities defaced by these expressions of rage. It costs America more than $8 billion per year just to clean up graffiti.

There are four primary motivating factors for graffiti vandalism: fame, rebellion, self-expression, and power. Likewise, there are four types of graffiti: tagging, satanic/hate, gang, and generic (non-threatening messages like "Bobby loves Suzy" or "Class of 2000"). Nita City mainly deals with gang and tagging graffiti. Tagging graffiti is more ornate, while gang graffiti uses symbols. Regardless of the type, all forms of graffiti are against the law.

Graffiti is symbolic language. Many of the markings of gangs are symbols, and they have symbolic meaning for gang members. Some of these symbols are so meaningful that disrespecting the graffiti can be lethal for the person who paints over it or shows disrespect in some other way. Graffiti has been called the newspaper or bulletin board for gangs. It communicates many messages, including challenges, warnings, and pronouncements of deeds accomplished or about to occur. For example, graffiti will tell which gang members are in the area; relationships between males and females; a gang member showing disrespect to another person; the role call (a roster of gang members); the hierarchy of gang members in a gang; the strength of the gang; which gangs are claiming specific territory and which areas are in dispute. It may also be an advertisement for the type of activity in which the gang was or is still involved (including criminal behaviors). It also announces when a gang is getting ready to attack another gang or individual (a moniker or gang member's name that is crossed out with an "X" is the likely target for an attack or murder) or if someone has already been killed.

According to the National Council to Prevent Delinquency (NCPD), about 80 percent of graffiti is hip-hop or "tagger" graffiti. Another 5 percent are "pieces." Nationally, gang graffiti makes up about 10 percent.

A "tag" is the graffiti vandal's moniker applied quickly and repetitively. A tagger writes his or her nickname ("tag") so that it will be seen by his or her peers. Tags can be recognized by their particular style, which consists only of the tagger and/or crew name. Tag names are typically one short word, like "BUSTER," and crew names are usually three or four initials, such as "RLP." Taggers thrive on placing their tag names on as many places as possible. They also look for dangerous places. A "throw-up" is a more elaborate tag, usually done in two or more colors. Vandals often use balloon letters, which are filled in or left as outlines. "Pieces," short for "masterpieces," are large, detailed drawings. They are colorful, can include cartoon-like characters, and may take an hour or more to complete.

When deciphering graffiti, one should begin by looking at the letters, if any, and the overall design. If it has "bubble letters," more than one color of paint or ink, or shows even a hint of artistry, it is usually not gang related. If it has sharp, angular stick letters, or contains religious (including "satanic") imagery, or is done in one color of paint, it is more likely to be gang related.

Many times graffiti is quite easy to understand, e.g. the statement "West Side Bloods." That, obviously, is easy to figure out. Gang graffiti can often be a series of letters or numbers that don't seem to make any immediate sense.

Beginning with numbers, if there is more than one digit, especially 13, 14, or 18, it is most likely graffiti for a Hispanic gang. Two digits prefixed by "N," "S," "E," or "W" (or "NS," "SS," "ES," or "WS") relate to the cardinal directions and form part of the gang's identity. Three digits, especially corresponding to the local area code, suggests it is not a Hispanic gang, but a more typical prison or street gang.

If the numbers are followed by "K," it suggests a threat from a rival gang—a trailing "K" is a threat to "(K)ill", as are any crossed-out letters. An "A" at the very beginning pretty much always stands for "Almighty." Likewise, if the tag ends with an "N," that virtually always stands for "Nation." Those two usually occur together, and show up surprisingly often, as pretty much every two-bit bunch of street thugs takes to calling themselves the Almighty Whatever Nation.

There are a pretty finite number of identified gangs in this country, and it's fairly easy to recognize the abbreviations for most of the most common ones. Those include "GD," standing for the Gangster Disciples, for example; "VL" are the Vice Lords. "LK" are the Latin Kings, and "LQ" the Latin Queens; sometimes, when they are getting along, they are the LKQ—Latin Kings and Queens. Extending the process to include all of the possible letters, you may see ALKQN (Almighty Latin Kings and Queens Nation).

Earlier, I referenced a difference in stylistic presentation of the message. Stylized lettering, multiple colors, and connected artwork suggest this is tagging and not gang messaging. While I do not see a difference between a tagger and a gang member, taggers think of themselves as artists. While their graffiti may be artful, it also represents an act of vandalism, since they often post their art on public property—sides of buses and trains, sides of commercial businesses, walls, etc. It may well become a significant territorial marker or billboard for an area gang—regardless of whether the "writer" is an actual member of a specific gang.

Taggers, or "writers," may also be employed by street gangs to convey messages. In these cases, the message may take on the appearance of the more ornate "Urban Art." It would be easy for residents of an area to become confused as to whether graffiti is "Urban Art" or a gang message.

In some parts of the country, taggers have started to mimic gangs by becoming increasingly violent. Besides stealing most of the materials they use to tag (it is illegal to sell spray paint to minors), many vandals have started to carry weapons to protect themselves from gangs or rival tagging crews. This alarming new phenomenon is called "tag-banging," and while it is widespread in some cities, it is not yet common in Nita City. The department is concerned that this will become a new type of crime within the city. We are closely observing tagging crews like Modern Neighborhood Art to make sure they do not move towards violence. If they do, we will shut them down quickly.

You specifically asked me to comment on graffiti by Modern Neighborhood Art, or MNA. In the area in close proximity to Nita Gardens there is a significant amount of graffiti done by this group of taggers. This leads me to believe that one or more of the members of this tagger crew, or gang, live in that building. My intelligence tells me that Elroy Johnson is the leader of the group called MNA. While I do not have concrete proof of this, it is true the information I have is quite reliable. In studying the tags of MNA I would tell you it is my opinion that they are not related to the Vice Lords street gang. The messages spelled out in the examples I viewed were not gang-related messages.

Even if the work of MNA is not gang-related graffiti, it does not suggest that these pieces of graffiti are legal. Each of them was clearly a violation of Nita City's anti-graffiti laws. They are vandalism and foster a sense of fear and intimidation with residents or the area. I spoke with a number of locals about the graffiti in the area. Many of the adults indicated they could not see a difference between the gang graffiti and the tagging. The significant presence of the Vice Lords in this neighborhood has created great concern for the health, safety, and right to peaceful enjoyment of all community members, especially those who live in Nita Gardens. All of the area graffiti suggests gang activity to these residents, and they are quite scared. The tagging by Elroy Johnson and Modern Neighborhood Art plays a significant role in the discomfort of local residents. In my expert opinion, this graffiti has a substantial negative impact on resident's feelings of health and safety and affects their rights to peaceful enjoyment of their homes.

I would be happy to repeat my opinion in open court if it would be of assistance to you. Please feel free to call on me should it become necessary.

Sincerely,

James T. Wherder

Lt. James T. Wherder

Gang Task Force

LT. JAMES T. WHERDER
Nita City Police Department
Gang Task Force
1 Police Center
Nita City, Nita

Education

- Criminal Justice AAS Degree, Arapahoe Community College, Denver, Colorado, YR-24

- Bachelor of Science Degree, Criminology, Nita State University, YR-17

- Masters of Arts Degree, Anthropology, University of Nita, YR-5

- Master Thesis - *The Use of Graffiti in Gang Activities*

Experience

- United States Army, Special Troops Battalion, 3rd Brigade Combat Team, 10th Mountain Division. Military Police Team Leader. YR-24 to YR-19. Rank: Sergeant.
  - Assigned as a Police Mentor Team Leader in advising local police in Saudi Arabia. Provided training to local police in handling firearms, handcuffing suspects, making vehicle stops, and carrying out searches.

- Nita City Police Department. YR-20 to present. Rank: Lieutenant.
  - YR-20 to YR-9   6th Police District.
    - Assigned as Street Patrol Officer.
  - YR-9 - present   Gang Task Force
    - Commanding officer of Gang Task Force. Working with community organizations to prevent gang activity within Nita City. Community relations relating to gangs, graffiti, and youth activities. Criminal investigations relating to drug sales, extortion, prostitution, and gang-related violence.

Citations

- YR-15   Citation for valor

- YR-10   Citation for community service

- YR-5   Citation for community service

- YR-2   Special Citation for Mayor's Task Force on Gang Activity

Courses Taught

- YR-7 to present   Nita City Police Academy. Youth Gangs; Graffiti & Tagging; Interpretation of Gang Signs and Graffiti.

- YR-3 to present   Nita City Community College, Department of Criminology. Introduction to Criminology; Street Gangs; Asian Gangs and Organized Crime; Outlaw Motorcycle Gangs;

- YR-1 to present   Police National Training Institute. The Gang Phenomena; Into the Abyss: Training a Gang Unit; Graffiti & Tagging.

Presentations

- March 21, YR-1   *Larry King Live*, CNBC. Interview with Mr. King on Gang Activity, Gang Signs, and Graffiti.

- October 12, YR-4   *News 4 Nita*, Helpline on bullying, gangs, and drugs.

- January 21, YR-5   *Take Back Our Streets*. Mayor's Symposium on Gang Activity in Nita City.

Exhibit 1

Selected portions of Johnson lease

NITA CITY HOUSING AUTHORITY
PUBLIC HOUSING LEASE

1. DESCRIPTION OF THE PARTIES AND PREMISES

The Nita City Housing Authority (NCHA) hereby leases to (Tenant/Resident),

Ladonna Johnson   Apartment # *715-E*,

874 Jackson Avenue, (address), Nita City, Nita (the Apartment/Premises)

beginning *March 1, YR-5*.

2. AMOUNT AND DUE DATE OF RENTAL PAYMENTS

Resident agrees to pay the monthly rent of $ *169.00* in advance, on or before the fifth calendar day

of each month beginning *March 1, YR-5*. Rent for any fraction of a month of occupancy at the beginning or end of the term will be charged on a pro rata basis. This rent will remain in effect until changed in accordance with NCHA policy. NCHA agrees to accept rental payments without regard to any other charge owed by Resident to NCHA, and to seek separate legal remedy for collection of any such charge. NCHA agrees to accept monthly rental payments in two (2) installments if Resident shows, in advance and in writing, good cause for the request. Resident agrees that acceptance of payments by NCHA shall not constitute a waiver of any claims made.

NCHA shall pay the full cost of the following utilities:

Natural gas for heating

Electricity

Water, sewer, and garbage collection

Resident shall pay the full cost of the following utilities:

Telephone

Cable television

Resident shall pay additional monthly charges for use of resident-supplied major appliances (for example, dryers, freezers) to the extent permitted by applicable NCHA policy. The following are the monthly charges for resident-supplied appliances; the addition of other major appliances will result in additional charges.

Appliance Charges *Freezer @ $5 every two months*

3. TERM OF LEASE; ANNUAL AND INTERIM REDETERMINATIONS

For residents in state-subsidized housing, the term of this Lease begins on the date first written above and continues until terminated pursuant to Section 9 of this Lease. For residents in federally-subsidized housing, the term of this Lease begins on the date first written above and continues for one year. Annually the lease will automatically be renewed for an additional one-year term, subject to Resident's compliance, and the compliance by members of Resident's household, with the provisions of NCHA's Community Service Policy and 42 U.S.C. 1437j(c). In the event of failure by Resident or any non-exempt adult member of Resident's household to cure noncompliance of this requirement within the period and in the manner specified by NCHA's Community Service Policy and 42 U.S.C. 1437j(c), NCHA will not renew this Lease and will proceed to evict the household pursuant to Paragraph 9(E), below. All provisions of this Lease related to NCHA's Community Service Policy that are not in effect at the time this Lease is executed will go into effect and become binding upon the Parties once said Community Service Policy is adopted, and after thirty days' notice by NCHA to Resident that such Policy has been adopted and its provisions are in effect.

* * *

7. NCHA OBLIGATIONS

NCHA will at all times and at NCHA's expense

A. Permit Resident quietly and peaceably to enjoy the leased premises, respecting Resident's right to privacy;

B. Not interfere with Resident's constitutional rights to organize or join a tenant organization;

C. Notify Resident, in writing, of the specific grounds for any proposed adverse action against Resident by NCHA, and notify Resident of Resident's right to request a hearing and the time period in which to make such a hearing request if NCHA's grievance procedure requires the NCHA to afford Resident the opportunity for a hearing;

D. Commence eviction proceedings against other residents or their household members, whose own conduct or the conduct of their guests has jeopardized the health or safety of Resident, household members, other NCHA residents, or of NCHA employees. . . .

8. RESIDENT OBLIGATIONS

During the term of this lease, Resident agrees to

A. Conduct himself/herself, and cause other household members and any persons who are on or about the premises with his or her consent to conduct themselves, in a manner that will not disturb any other resident's or neighbor's peaceful enjoyment of his or her accommodations; will not harass, injure, endanger, threaten, or unreasonably disturb any other resident, any NCHA employee, or any other person lawfully in the unit or on the NCHA's property or residing in the immediate vicinity of the NCHA's property; will not cause damage; and that will be conducive to maintaining the development in a decent, safe, and sanitary condition;

B. Conduct himself/herself, and cause other household members and any persons who are on or about the Premises with Resident's consent to conduct themselves, in a manner that will not violate the civil rights of any other resident, guest, NCHA employee, or other person lawfully on NCHA property;

C. Refrain from engaging in, and cause members of Resident's household, any guest, or any other person under Resident's control to refrain from engaging in, any criminal or illegal activity including

(1) Any criminal, illegal, or other activity that threatens the health, safety, or right to peaceful enjoyment of public housing premises by another residents or a NCHA employee, or that threatens the health or safety of any person residing in the immediate vicinity of the public housing premises;

(2) Any violent or drug-related criminal activity on or off NCHA property, or any activity resulting in a felony conviction;

D. Abide by all reasonable policies promulgated by NCHA for the benefit and well-being of the housing development and all the residents;

E. Certify annually that he/she has received a copy of the NCHA's "Zero Tolerance Policy" (the "Policy"), understands it, agrees with the terms of the Policy, and will cause other household members and any persons who are on or about the Premises with Resident's permission to comply with the Policy.

9. TERMINATION / NON-RENEWAL OF LEASE

A. This lease may be terminated by Resident at any time by giving thirty (30) days' written notice.

B. This lease may not be terminated by NCHA except for one of the following reasons:

(1) Nonpayment of rent;

(2) Commission by the Resident, a member of Resident's household, a guest, or other person under Resident's control, of

(a) Any criminal or other activity that threatens the health or safety of another resident or a NCHA employee, or that threatens his or her rights to peaceful enjoyment of public housing premises, or that threatens the health or safety of any person residing in the immediate vicinity of the public housing premises;

(b) Any violent or drug-related criminal activity on or off NCHA property;

(3) Interference with the health, safety, or right to peaceful enjoyment of NCHA property by another resident, due to illegal use or pattern of illegal use of a controlled substance or abuse or pattern of abuse of alcohol by Resident or member of Resident's household;

(4) Violation of any of the material terms of this lease;

(5) Material failure to comply with any decision of the NCHA's Grievance Panel;

C. The NCHA shall give written notice of lease termination in all cases. The notice shall be given the following periods in advance of termination:

(1) Ten (10) days in the case of failure to pay rent;

(2) A reasonable time considering the seriousness of the grounds for termination (but not to exceed thirty (30) days) when the health or safety of other tenant(s), NCHA employee(s), or person(s) residing in the immediate vicinity of the premises is threatened; or in the event of any drug-related or violent criminal activity or any felony conviction; and (3) Thirty (30) days in any other case.

D. The written notice of lease termination shall state specific grounds for termination, shall inform Resident of Resident's rights to make such reply as Resident shall wish, to examine relevant NCHA documents in Resident's file concerning the termination, and to request a hearing in accordance with NCHA's grievance procedure if NCHA's grievance procedure requires the NCHA to afford Resident the opportunity. In cases where the NCHA annuls and makes void this lease as authorized by N.R.S. §139, §19, the notice shall state the specific grounds for the termination, shall specify that eviction shall proceed in court under N.R.S. §239 or by commencing action for declaratory judgment as provided in N.R.S. §139, §19, and that HUD has determined that these eviction procedures contain the elements of basic due process.

E. If lease of Resident in federally subsidized housing expires and is not renewed due to Resident's failure to comply with, or the failure of any member of Resident's household to comply with, NCHA's Community Service Policy and 42 U.S.C. 1437j(c), NCHA shall give Resident thirty (30) days' notice to vacate, as well as notice terminating Resident's participation in the federal housing program. Such action shall be subject to NCHA's Grievance Procedures and Policy. If NCHA's action is upheld by the Grievance Panel, NCHA shall proceed to recover possession of Premises in accordance with N.R.S. §239.

10. LEGAL NOTICES

A. Any notice to Resident required by law or provided for in this lease, except such notices as provided in paragraph 13, shall be sufficient, and Resident agrees it shall constitute proper notice, if

(1) in writing; and

(2) (a) sent by first-class mail, properly stamped and addressed, to the Resident at his or her address with a proper return address;

(b) given to any adult person answering the door at the Apartment and mailing a copy;

(c) if no adult responds, by placing the notice under or through the door, if possible, and mailing a copy; or

(d) by such other means of service permitted by applicable law.

B. Notice to NCHA shall be sufficient if

(1) in writing; and

(2) delivered to the local management office or sent by first-class mail to the development manager at the local management office.

11. LEGAL COSTS

All legal costs, fees, and charges authorized by law and actually incurred by NCHA in connection with any court action brought against Resident will be charged to Resident, and Resident hereby agrees to pay the same if the NCHA prevails in court. Legal costs, fees, and charges shall include all court costs and other expenses incident to the court action.

12. GRIEVANCE PROCEDURE

All grievances arising under this lease may be resolved in accordance with NCHA's then-applicable Grievance Procedures and Policy.

13. AUTHORIZED FAMILY MEMBERS

Except as otherwise provided by a written Lease Addendum, the individuals listed below shall be the only persons authorized to occupy the Apartment with Resident and shall comprise the Resident's household. If more than one party signs this lease as Resident, the agreements of Resident shall be the joint and several obligations of all such parties, and references to Resident shall include all such parties.

Elroy Johnson, 11 years old - grandson

Sara Johnson, 13 years old - granddaughter

IN WITNESS WHEREOF, the parties have executed this lease agreement this *17* day of

April YR-5, at Nita City, Nita

Ladonna Johnson

(Resident)

Rachel Longly

(Nita City Housing Authority)
Title: Administrator/Manager, Nita Gardens
NCHA Lease Rev. Jan. 2000

Exhibit 2

Nita City Police Department
Offense Report

File #:   Month-10 - 1280
Offense: Possession of controlled substance; sale of controlled substance; conspiracy to sell controlled substance
Victim: N/A
Location: Nita Gardens Public Housing, 874 Jackson Avenue, Nita City, Nita parking lot surrounding building
Date: Month 10,
By: Detective Roberta Behmer—Gang Task Force

On Month-10, 5, at approximately 1300, I received a call from a reliable confidential informant that a street gang, the Vice Lords, was using the parking lot at Nita Gardens to sell crack cocaine. The informant told me that he had arranged to purchase several rocks of crack from one Jerry Collins on Month-10, 8 at 1930.

Based on this information, I assembled a strike force from the Gang Task Force to conduct a raid at the time of the proposed sale. Included in the strike force were Detectives Wasilewski and Taggert and Officers Smith, Fredericks, Robinson, and Gardini. Additional street units were secured from the 12th Precinct station.

On Month-10, 8, at approximately 1700, units were deployed to the location at 874 Jackson Avenue and the surrounding area. These included two unmarked vans, two marked cruisers, and a command unit. Confidential informant (name redacted) was with the strike force and was equipped with a radio transmitter.

At 1905, a large group of people, later identified as suspects, emerged from the front entrance of Nita Gardens and congregated in the parking lot under a street light. Observation indicated that the group was twenty in number, including both male and female subjects of varying ages from teen to young adult. Subjects appeared to be in conversation.

At 1920 informant exited command vehicle and walked to subjects. Radio transmitter was intermittent and failed within five minutes. Command switched to direct observation of informant.

At approximately 1930, what appeared to be a transaction occurred between informant and member of group, later identified as Jerry Collins. I ordered officers to surround group and apprehend perpetrators. Four police vehicles proceeded into parking lot. Some of the group attempted to flee, but were captured by officers.

Search of Jerry Collins and others in group found amounts of suspected drugs and drug paraphernalia. Decision was made to arrest all parties in the group. I called for sheriff's bus to transport suspects to 12th Precinct station for processing and interviewing. Bus arrived at approximately 2045.

Upon arrival at 12th Precinct station, Detectives Wasilewski and Taggert and I began processing prisoners. Decision was made to charge each prisoner with one or all of the following drug-related offenses: possession of a controlled substance, possession with intent to sell a controlled substance, or conspiracy to sell a controlled substance.

Processing of detained prisoners completed at 0120 on Month-10, 9. The following individuals were booked at that time:

1. Jerry Collins   Possession, possession with intent to sell, conspiracy to sell
2. Albert Decalbe   Possession, possession with intent to sell, conspiracy to sell, resisting arrest
3. Derrick Colby   Conspiracy to sell
4. Jeffery White   Conspiracy to sell, possession of drug paraphernalia
5. Daniel Rose   Conspiracy to sell
6. Harmony Sampson   Conspiracy to sell, possession of drug paraphernalia
7. Elroy Johnson   Conspiracy to sell
8. Marcus Horton   Conspiracy to sell
9. Francis Jay   Conspiracy to sell, possession of a concealed weapon
10. Bruce Brown   Conspiracy to sell, resisting arrest
11. Sheila Elbert   Conspiracy to sell
12. Ernie Jones   Conspiracy to sell
13. Aaron Bell   Conspiracy to sell, attempted escape
14. James Hollis   Conspiracy to sell, possession of drug paraphernalia
15. Douglas Frist   Conspiracy to sell
16. June Scruggs   Conspiracy to sell
17. Geoff Ray   Conspiracy to sell, possession of a concealed weapon
18. Michael Brownlee   Conspiracy to sell
19. Derek Mason   Conspiracy to sell
20. Andre Upshaw   Conspiracy to sell, possession of graffiti paraphernalia

Month-10, 9: Detectives Wasilewski and Taggert; Assistant District Attorneys Melanie Gonzales, Michael Burton, and Steven Colgate; and I met with each prisoner to advise them of their rights and to interview. Several prisoners declined to speak without the presence of counsel. Others waived their rights and spoke.

Month-10, 9: Charges dismissed against Derrick Colby, Daniel Rose, Marcus Horton, Sheila Elbert, Ernie Jones, Douglas Frist, June Scruggs, Michael Brownlee, and Derek Mason. Plea agreements reached with Jeffery White, Harmony Sampson, Bruce Brown, Elroy Johnson, Aaron Bell, James Hollis, Geoff Ray, and Andre Upshaw.

Submitted by:

Roberta Behmer

Det. Roberta Behmer

Exhibit 2a

Transcript of Grand Jury Meeting – Month-10, 20 Testimony of Elroy Johnson

District Attorney Burton questioning:

Mr. Johnson, you are now under oath and have sworn to tell the truth in this matter. You are here today to tell the ladies and gentlemen of the Grand Jury what you know about events occurring on the evening of Month-10, 8. Your truthful statement and cooperation are part of an agreement with this office to dismiss charges against you.

Burton: What is your name and address?

Johnson: Elroy Johnson. I live at Nita Gardens, 874 Jackson Avenue, Apartment 715-E, Nita City.

Q: You understand that you are under oath. Your statements today are the truth, and anything you say today may be used in other proceedings. Anything you say today that is not truthful may be used against you in the future.

A: I understand what you have said and promise to tell the truth.

Q: Your statements today are being made with the understanding that you will cooperate with any future prosecution of members of Vice Lords. As a result of your statements, we have agreed to dismiss all charges brought against you in relation to the events of Month-10, 8.

A: I understand.

Q: You may begin your statement.

A: I want to be sure everyone understands that I am not a member of the street gang the Vice Lords and that I do not do drugs. I do hang out with people who are members of the Vice Lords. I know that some of them are on drugs. I also know that some of the members of the Vice Lords sell drugs to others.

Jerry Collins and Albert Decalbe are the two members of the Vice Lords who I know sell the drugs. They are very tough guys—serious gangsters. If anyone wants to score some coke or crack, they are the ones to see in my neighborhood.

At first I just thought Jerry and Albert were cool dudes. They always had spending cash, and lots of folks wanted to hang with them. The finest looking ladies were always to be found with those two. It made you feel like you were special if they would let you hang with them. I started playing basketball with that crew around the school. Then we naturally moved to the gym at Nita Gardens. I didn't know they were dealing drugs when I first met them. When I found out they had used me as a way to use Nita Gardens as a place to deal, it was too late for me to do anything about it. Those two are seriously bad dudes. Folks get hurt bad or just plain disappear when Jerry takes a dislike to them. I knew that if I said anything about their selling drugs, my days would be numbered.

I've seen both Jerry and Albert sell drugs in the parking lot outside Nita Gardens more than once. I've heard they occasionally sell inside the building as well. I don't know who they are selling to inside the building, and I've never seen that happen.

On the evening of Month 10, 8, I was playing basketball with those guys from about 6:00 to 7:00. We finished our game and everyone went outside to hang in the parking lot. Mostly people were just talking and messing around. I was getting ready to go back inside to do my homework, but Frankie—that's Francis Jay—told me to stay put because Jerry needed to get some business done before the group broke up. At about 7:20 this guy comes over to the group and starts talking to Jerry. I see him pass some money to Jerry and get a bag of crack in return. That's when the police all showed up and arrested everyone.

I also want everyone to understand that I do not write for the Vice Lords. I have never tagged anything either as a favor or for hire by the Vice Lords.

I want to make sure that if I have to go to court you will protect me and my family. I'm really scared of those dudes and others in the Vice Lords. I won't talk if they threaten my Gram or sister.

Exhibit 3

State of Nita
Uniform Arrest and Disposition Record

Name: Elroy Johnson   DOB: 8/20/YR-16

SS: 164-39-2087   POB: Nita City, Nita

Date: Month-10, 8

Address: 874 Jackson Ave., Nita City, NI

Offense: Conspiracy to sell

Disposition: Dismissed (agreed to testify in case # YR-0, 1025)

John Schnek

John Schnek

Notary Public

Carolyn Brownlee

Superintendent of Documents

Exhibit 4

Notice to Grievance Committee

To:	Nita Gardens Grievance Panel
From:	Ladonna Johnson
Subject:	Eviction
Date:	Month-3, 8, YR-0

Under the terms of my lease, I am entitled to participate in any Tenant Action Committee without fear of actions by the building management. I was given notice of eviction claiming my grandson was involved in criminal and drug activities. This is false!

The real reason for my eviction was my formation of a Tenant Action Committee for the purpose of forcing management to install a fire sprinkler system. The building manager is using the arrest of my grandson, Elroy, as an excuse. Elroy had charges dismissed and has not been involved in criminal activity. The building claims he is part of an illegal street gang. He is not a member of any gang.

I insist that my lease be reinstated at the same monthly rent.

Ladonna Johnson

Exhibit 5

Nita Gardens

April 1, YR-1

Ms. Ladonna Johnson
Nita Gardens - Apartment 715-E
Nita City, Nita

Dear Ms. Johnson:

Under the terms of your lease, Nita Gardens must provide to you a copy of the Nita City Housing Authority Zero Tolerance Policy each year. You are to review the policy and then must agree with the terms of the policy. In addition, it is your responsibility to cause other members of your household and your guests who are on or about the premises to comply with the policy.

Attached is a copy of the Zero Tolerance Policy. Kindly read the policy, share it with others in your household, and then sign the bottom of this letter and return it to me no later than ten days from now. If you fail to sign, date, and return this form within ten days you are in breach of your lease and your lease may be terminated.

Thank you.

Sincerely,

Rachel Longly

Ms. Rachel Longly
Building Manager

X   I have read the Nita City Housing Authority Zero Tolerance Policy, I agree with the policy, and will follow that policy.

___   I do not agree with the Zero Tolerance Policy and understand my lease will be terminated.

Signed: *Ladonna Johnson*   Print your name: Ladonna Johnson

Date: April 10, YR-1

Nita City Housing Authority Zero Tolerance Policy

(As of 1 January YR-23)

The NCHA has established a zero tolerance policy for any criminal activity that threatens the health, safety, or right to peaceful enjoyment of the premises by other tenants or, for any drug-related criminal activity on or off such premises.

Under this Policy, a resident's entire household will be subject to eviction if the resident, any member of the resident's household, any guest, or any other person under the resident's control, is involved in any criminal activity that violates the health, safety, or right to peaceful enjoyment of the premises, or is involved in any drug-related criminal activity on or off such premises.

Any such activities shall be cause for the immediate termination of tenancy on Authority property.

This Policy applies to all residents, who are required to sign a certification that they agree to comply with the Zero Tolerance Policy.

Exhibit 6

Nita Gardens

Month-2, 7, YR-0

Ms. Ladonna Johnson
Nita Gardens - Apartment 715-E
Nita City, Nita
RE: Your eviction

Dear Ms. Johnson:

The Grievance Panel met yesterday evening. Your petition was considered by the members of the panel. After a review of all of the facts, the panel has determined your eviction is in keeping with the terms of the lease and state and federal law.

You are hereby notified that your petition has been dismissed, and you are to vacate the premises as set forth in the notice of eviction.

Phyllis Crabtree
Phyllis Crabtree

Chairwoman, Nita Gardens Grievance Panel

Exhibit 7

Nita Gardens Public Housing

Exhibit 8

Nita Gardens Public Housing

Elroy Johnson and companions arrested here

Location of Ladonna Johnson's apartment

Exhibit 9

Gang-Related Graffitti near Nita Gardens

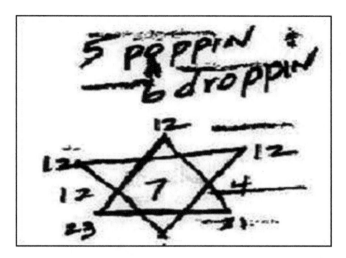

Example 1: Found on the walls of Frederick's Garage at 1528 Main Street, Nita City, on 8/20/YR-1.
Tied to the Vice Lords

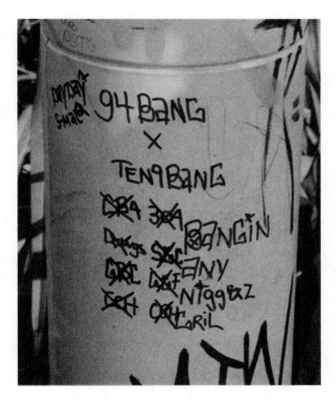

Example 2: Found on the street light one block south of Nita Gardens, Nita City, on 10/5/YR-1.
Found to be Vice Lords graffiti.

Exhibit 10

Examples of Modern Neighborhood Art Tagger Graffiti

Example 1: Wall mural found on the wall of private apartment building, 1639 Jefferson Street (located six blocks from Nita Gardens).

Example 2: Good/Evil tag photographed on wall of Nita Gardens, 7/21/YR-2.

Example 3: Wall art found on the parking lot wall of Quick-Mart, 1734 Centennial Ave. (six blocks from Nita Gardens) on 6/6/YR-1.

Exhibit 11

NITA FIRE DEPARTMENT

Residential Automatic Fire Sprinklers

How Automatic Sprinklers Work

Automatic sprinkler systems supply water to a network of individual sprinklers, each protecting an area below them. These sprinklers open automatically in response to high heat and spray water on a fire to put it out or keep it from spreading. Contrary to popular belief, only those sprinklers above or near the fire operate and spray water.

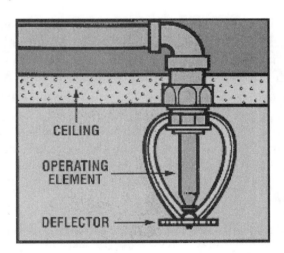

Sprinklers Save Lives

National Fire Protection Association (NFPA) records covering most of this century show no instances of fires killing three or more people in a house, apartment, hotel, or motel where a complete sprinkler system was installed and operating properly.

The NFPA estimates that the risk of dying in a fire is cut by up to two-thirds in public buildings, stores, offices, auditoriums, and factories where sprinklers have been installed. This also holds true in the growing number of private homes equipped with sprinkler systems.

Because sprinkler systems act so early in the course of a fire, they reduce not only the heat and flames, but also the amount of smoke produced in a fire. Everything a fire produces that threatens life is reduced by sprinklers.

Sprinklers Save Property

NFPA studies show that, in a fire, automatic sprinkler systems also save thousands of dollars in property loss. The cost of fire damage in a sprinkled home is statistically much lower—up to 75 percent less. In addition, a sprinkler system installed in many properties can pay for itself over time through reduced insurance premiums.

Sprinklers in the Home

Four-fifths of all fire deaths occur in homes, and according to a study by the National Institute of Standards Technology 60 to 70 percent of those deaths could be prevented by adding sprinkler systems to houses and apartments.

Automatic sprinkler systems have been common in factories, warehouses, hotels, and public buildings throughout the twentieth century. Since the early 1980s, sprinklers have also become more popular in private homes, thanks to increased education and revised standards for installation that have made home sprinkler systems practical and affordable.

Thanks also to the use of modern materials and designs, the cost of residential sprinkler systems has come down. Estimates suggest that installing such a system would only add one to one and a half percent to the cost of new housing. These systems can be supplied with water through small diameter piping from a household water supply in one or two-family dwellings. Automatic sprinklers can also be installed in existing buildings; however, the cost in general would be greater.

Homes with automatic sprinkler systems should also be equipped with smoke detectors, as this will provide an even greater level of protection and thereby reduce damages and injuries from fire. All residents should be familiar with these devices and should have a plan for escape in the event of fire.

Dispelling Myths About Automatic Sprinklers

Despite the proven effectiveness of automatic sprinkler systems in slowing the spread of fire and reducing loss of life and property damage, many people resist the idea of home sprinkler systems because of widespread misconceptions about their operation.

Myth: The water damage from sprinklers is worse than a fire.

The truth is a sprinkler will control a fire with a tiny fraction of the water used by fire department hoses, primarily because it acts so much earlier. Automatic systems spray water only in the immediate area of the fire and can keep the fire from spreading, thus avoiding widespread water damage.

Myth: Sprinklers go off accidentally, causing unnecessary water damage.

Accidental water damage caused by automatic sprinkler systems is relatively rare. One study concluded that sprinkler accidents are generally less likely and less severe than mishaps involving standard home plumbing systems.

Myth: Sprinklers are ugly.

Sprinklers don't have to be unattractive. Pipes can be hidden behind ceilings or walls, and modern sprinklers can be inconspicuous—mounted almost flush with walls or ceilings. Some sprinklers can even be concealed.

Installation

Residential and commercial automatic sprinkler systems must be installed by a qualified contractor. For a list of local qualified contractors, see our list of Sprinkler Contractors.

For any additional questions about fire sprinkler systems, please contact the Nita Fire Prevention Bureau at (555) 257-9590.

Exhibit 12

Arts & Letters
Month-2, 9

Nita City Professor Recreates NYC Subway Art Revival in the Heart of Downtown

Professor Anne Worthington Stockbridge of the University of Nita is on a mission. As Professor of Art History and Urban Studies, Ms. Stockbridge has begun a campaign to recreate urban art, known to many as graffiti that was once painted on subway cars in the New York City transit system. The project will also highlight new urban art from a local group of graffiti artists.

According to Professor Stockbridge, "The idea is to use these pieces to try to teach a two-part history lesson. The first is about the glories (as Stockbridge and her team of graffiti artists see it) of the early days of graffiti and the invention of a vernacular art form that has swept the world. The second lesson is about world history itself, in neighborhoods where education remains low on the list of priorities for many

struggling teenagers. We are taking art originally published in the landmark photographic history **Subway Art** by Henry Chalfant and Martha Cooper and putting a local spin on those masterpieces of urban art."

"Some of our changes convert some of the more ominous symbols to a gentler and more philosophic rendition," said Stockbridge.

An example of one of the original pieces of Urban Art that Stockbridge's group has edited to be less ominous.

"Converting images and making allusions to warriors, philosophers, and characters from Western and Eastern mythology plus current writers, artists, and political and religious figures is our way of helping to educate teens who are not always interested in school."

"We hope that the people who see the words in these new urban art pieces help each other figure out what they are about, and that these things start a conversation that keeps on going on the streets." said one of Stockbridge's artists, Elroy Johnson.

Professor Stockbridge and her "crew" of urban artists are getting permission from property owners, businesses, schools, and other "nostalgic" owners of blank vertical space in the inner parts of Nita City.

The group is modeling their project on a similar one going on in New York City. "'Subway Art History' gave me the idea that we could educate the people of Nita City that urban art is not a blight but one of the newest and most politically expressive forms of art. Urban artists can help to beautify parts of our city while subtly teaching and offering political expression. All too often urban artists run afoul of the law as they attempt to express themselves. We are using this project to work cooperatively with those who own the

'canvas' and thwart police attempts to stifle the creativity of these young men and women," offered Stockbridge.

Johnson, a former graffiti writer who helped Professor Stockbridge to form the collective group of artists now painting in Nita City, said, "In graffiti it's like a teenage thing: 'No way am I going to become the man, no way am I going to make anything that looks like anyone else's'—and then, of course, you become the man." Johnson asked that the other names of the tagging crew (there is a floating membership of approximately 10 writers) be withheld, not for the usual reason—the police —but because the group is seeking to get away from the ego-jockeying that normally accompanies graffiti work. "It's like a real-life Wikipedia project that uses the streets."

Prints made from several of the new murals will begin being sold next week as part of "Graffiti Reborn," a new online art gallery that sells limited edition prints and gives the proceeds to Nita City homeless charities. Professor Stockbridge hopes to compile photographs of all of the pieces, which could take more than a year, into a book.

THIS ARTICLE IS A TAKE-OFF OF "NOW EVERYONE CAN READ THE WRITING ON THE WALL," AN ARTICLE BY RANDY KENNEDY PUBLISHED IN THE ARTS SECTION OF THE NEW YORK TIMES ON WEDNESDAY, OCTOBER 27, 2010, C1.

Nita City Mural Call for Peace
by Kathryn Richards/yourhub.nita
Month-1, 16, YR-0

Teens who once tagged are now painting positive messages

Elroy Johnson used to tag sides of buildings with his nickname and other art. The sixteen-year-old, who's been in trouble with the law for his graffiti habits since he was fourteen, is now tagging in a different sort of way. He is one of a handful of teens helping paint the latest peace mural in Nita City.

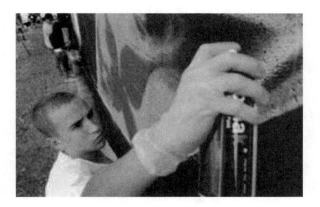

Eddie Franklin, formerly of the Tagger Group MNA,
working on a new mural in Nita City

The mural—which is receiving final touches today on the southwest corner of 16th Avenue and Jackson Street in the La Alma Park neighborhood—joins seven others citywide.

The murals are billed as messages of hope in communities often riddled with gang violence.

It's an initiative created by GRASP, or Gang Rescue and Support Project, an intervention program in Nita City that works with youth who are at risk of gang involvement or are presently in gangs. GRASP is the creation of Lt. James Wherder of the Nita City Police Department. Wherder is head of the Gang Task Force unit of the department.

The first mural, which went up in YR-1 in the Cole neighborhood, was a symbolic call to "cease fire" after a slew of gang killings in Nita City, said Johnny Santos, community outreach coordinator for GRASP.

"We tell the community, 'This is yours,'" Santos said. "They're billboards for our community for the love of our children. You rarely hear that."

Through GRASP and the Day Reporting Program—a Nita City juvenile probation program that allows teens on probation to go through an eight-week rehabilitation course instead of going to jail—teens, like Johnson, who were once the ones tagging, are now removing graffiti and able to prove their artistic abilities in other ways.

Elroy Johnson completing work on the "Peace" mural at 16th Street and Jackson.

"I'm doing community service by doing something I like to do," Johnson said. "I used to tag and this is giving me a way to do it legally and do something positive for the community."

The result is a 100-foot mural on the side of a building that's been painted and repainted to cover up graffiti. This mural is a tribute to the U.S., Nita, and Nita City's culture with images of the mountains and downtown painted across a giant film reel.

Once a mural is painted on a building that normally gets tagged, the taggers stop, Santos said.

"You never disrespect a mural," Johnson said. "That's just a common rule."

As for Johnson's future as a tagger, he said, "I'm not going to do it again because it will get me into worse trouble. It's not worth it."

When asked about the new GRASP graffiti project, Nita University Professor Anne Worthington Stockbridge commented, "It's nice to see the Nita City police finally recognize that Urban Art is the new inner city renaissance. While this program is a take-off on our own Urban Art project that recreates some of the most famous New York City subway art in new images, it is a start. For too long the Nita City government has refused to recognize that Urban Art is a form of political expression. Hopefully, this will signal a change in the archaic city laws prohibiting free speech in the form of graffiti.

Kathryn Richards: richardsk@yourhub.nita

SELECTED STATUTES

Nita Revised Statutes Title 13 Article 40—Forcible Entry and Detainer

13-40-103. Forcible Detention Prohibited

No person, having peaceably entered into or upon any real property without right to the possession thereof, shall forcibly hold or detain the same as against the person who has a lawful right to such possession.

13-40-106.5. Termination of Tenancy for Substantial Violation Definition—Legislative Declaration

(1) The general assembly finds and declares that:

    (a) Violent and antisocial criminal acts are increasingly committed by persons who base their operations in rented homes, apartments, and commercial properties;

    (b) Such persons often lease such property from owners who are unaware of the dangerous nature of such persons until after the persons have taken possession of the property;

    (c) Under traditional landlord and tenant law, such persons may have established the technical, legal right to occupy the premises for a fixed term, which continues long after they have demonstrated themselves unfit to coexist with their neighbors and cotenants; furthermore, such persons often resist eviction as long as possible;

    (d) In certain cases it is necessary to curtail the technical, legal right of occupancy of such persons in order to protect the equal or greater rights of neighbors and cotenants, the interests of property owners, the values of trust and community within neighborhoods, and the health, safety, and welfare of all the people of this state.

(2) It is declared to be an implied term of every lease of real property in this state that the tenant shall not commit a substantial violation while in possession of the premises.

(3) As used in this section, "substantial violation" means any act or series of acts by the tenant or any guest or invitee of the tenant that, when considered together:

    (a) Occurs on or near the premises and willfully and substantially endangers the property of the landlord, any cotenant, or any person living on or near the premises; or

    (b) Occurs on or near the premises and constitutes a violent or drug-related felony prohibited under Article 3, 4, 6, 7, 9, 10, 12, or 18 of Title 18, N.R.S.; or

    (c) Occurs on the tenant's leased premises or the common areas, hallway, grounds, parking lot, or other area located in the same building or complex in which the tenant's leased premises are located and constitutes a criminal act in violation of federal or state law or local ordinance that:

        (i) Carries a potential sentence of incarceration of 180 days or more; and

        (ii) Has been declared to be a public nuisance under state law or local ordinance based on a state statute.

(4) (a) A tenancy may be terminated at any time on the basis of a substantial violation. The termination shall be effective three days after service of written notice to quit.

(b) The notice to quit shall describe the property, the particular time when the tenancy will terminate, and the grounds for termination. The notice shall be signed by the landlord or by the landlord's agent or attorney.

(5) (a) In any action for possession under this section, the landlord has the burden of proving the occurrence of a substantial violation by a preponderance of the evidence.

(b) In any action for possession under this section, it shall be a defense that:

(i) (Deleted by amendment, L. 2005, p. 402, § 2, effective July 1, YR-5.)

(ii) The tenant did not know of, and could not reasonably have known of or prevented, the commission of a substantial violation by a guest or invitee but immediately notified a law enforcement officer of his or her knowledge of the substantial violation.

(c) (i) The landlord shall not have a basis for possession under this section if the tenant or lessee is the victim of domestic violence, as that term is defined in section 18-6-800.3, N.R.S., or of domestic abuse, as that term is defined in section 13-14-101 (2), N.R.S., which domestic violence or domestic abuse was the cause of or resulted in the alleged substantial violation and which domestic violence or domestic abuse has been documented pursuant to the provisions set forth in section 13-40-104 (4), N.R.S.

(ii) Nothing in this paragraph (c) shall prevent the landlord from seeking possession against a tenant or lessee of the premises who perpetuated the violence or abuse that was the cause of or resulted in the alleged substantial violation.

13-40-107. Service of Notice to Quit

A notice to quit or demand for possession of real property may be served by delivering a copy thereof to the tenant or other person occupying such premises, or by leaving such copy with some person, a member of the tenant's family above the age of fifteen years, residing on or in charge of the premises, or, in case no one is on the premises at the time service is attempted, by posting such copy in some conspicuous place on the premises.

13-40-115. Appeals

(1) If either party feels aggrieved by the judgment rendered in such action before the landlord/tenant court, he may appeal to the district court, as in other cases tried before the landlord/tenant court, with the additional requirements provided in this article.

(2) Upon the court's taking such appeal, all further proceedings in the case shall be stayed, and the appellate court shall thereafter issue all needful writs and process to carry out any judgment that may be rendered thereon in the appellate court.

(3) If the appellee believes that he may suffer serious economic harm during the pendency of the appeal, he may petition the court taking the appeal to order that an additional undertaking be required of the appellant to cover the anticipated harm. The court shall order such undertaking only after a hearing and upon a finding that the appellee has shown a substantial likelihood of suffering such economic harm during the pendency of the appeal and that he will not adequately be protected under the appeals bond and the other requirements for appeal pursuant to sections 13-40-118, 13-40-120, and 13-40-123.

13-40-122. Reprisal for reporting violations of law or for tenant's union activity; defense; presumption

It shall be a defense to an action for summary process that such action or the preceding action of terminating the tenant's tenancy, was taken against the tenant for the tenant's act of commencing, proceeding with, or obtaining relief in any judicial or administrative action the purpose of which action was to obtain damages, under or otherwise enforce, any federal, state, or local law, regulation, by-law, or ordinance, which has as its objective the regulation of residential premises, or exercising rights, or reporting a violation or suspected violation of law, or organizing or joining a tenants' union or similar organization, or making or expressing an intention to make a payment of rent to an organization of unit owners. The commencement of such action against a tenant, or the sending of a notice to quit upon which the summary process action is based, or the sending of a notice or performing any act the purpose of which is to materially alter the terms of the tenancy, within six months after the tenant has commenced, proceeded with or obtained relief in such action, exercised such rights, made such report, organized or joined such tenants' union, or made or expressed an intention to make a payment of rent to an organization of unit owners, or within six months after any other person has taken such action or actions on behalf of the tenant or relating to the building in which such tenant resides, shall create a rebuttable presumption that such summary process action is a reprisal against the tenant for engaging in such activities or was taken in the belief that the tenant had engaged in such activities. Such presumption may be rebutted only by clear and convincing evidence that such action was not a reprisal against the tenant and that the plaintiff had sufficient independent justification for taking such action, and would have in fact taken such action, in the same manner and at the same time the action was taken, even if the tenant had not commenced any legal action, made such report, or engaged in such activity.

History

Source: L. 1901: Entire article added, p. 271.

Nita Revised Statutes Title 18 Criminal Code: Article 23—

Gang Recruitment Act: 18-23-101—Definitions

18-23-101. Definitions.

As used in this article, unless the context otherwise requires

(1) "Criminal street gang" means any ongoing organization, association, or group of three or more persons, whether formal or informal:

    (a) That has as one of its primary objectives or activities the commission of one or more predicate criminal acts; and

    (b) Whose members individually or collectively engage in or have engaged in a pattern of criminal gang activity.

(2) "Pattern of criminal gang activity" means the commission, attempt, conspiracy, or solicitation of two or more predicate criminal acts that are committed on separate occasions or by two or more persons.

(3) "Predicate criminal acts" means the commission of or attempt, conspiracy, or solicitation to commit any of the following:

    (a) Any conduct defined as racketeering activity in section 18-17-103 (5);

(b) Any violation of section 18-8-706 or any criminal act committed in any jurisdiction of the United States that, if committed in this state, would violate section 18-8-706.

History

Source: L. 2001: Entire article added, p. 986, § 1, effective March 1, YR-10.

Nita Revised Statutes Title 18 Criminal Code Chapter 18-12-1-06

Criminal Attempt, Facilitation, Solicitation, Conspiracy

18-12-1-06-01. Criminal attempt.

(1) A person is guilty of criminal attempt if, acting with the kind of culpability otherwise required for commission of a crime, he intentionally engages in conduct that, in fact, constitutes a substantial step toward commission of the crime. A "substantial step" is any conduct that is strongly corroborative of the firmness of the actor's intent to complete the commission of the crime. Factual or legal impossibility of committing the crime is not a defense if the crime could have been committed had the attendant circumstances been as the actor believed them to be.

(2) A person who engages in conduct intending to aid another to commit a crime is guilty of criminal attempt if the conduct would establish his complicity under section 12-1-03-01 were the crime committed by the other person, even if the other is not guilty of committing or attempting the crime, for example, because he has a defense of justification or entrapment.

(3) Criminal attempt is an offense of the same class as the offense attempted, except that (a) an attempt to commit a class AA felony is a class A felony, and an attempt to commit a class A felony is a class B felony; and (b) whenever it is established by a preponderance of the evidence at sentencing that the conduct constituting the attempt did not come dangerously close to commission of the crime, an attempt to commit a class B felony shall be a class C felony, and an attempt to commit a class C felony shall be a class A misdemeanor.

History

Source: L. 1985: Entire article added, p. 2075, § 1, effective March 1, YR-27.

18-12-1-06-04. Criminal conspiracy.

(1) A person commits conspiracy if he agrees with one or more persons to engage in or cause conduct that, in fact, constitutes an offense or offenses, and any one or more of such persons does an overt act to effect an objective of the conspiracy. The agreement need not be explicit but may be implicit in the fact of collaboration or existence of other circumstances.

(2) If a person knows or could expect that one with whom he agrees, has agreed, or will agree with another to effect the same objective, he shall be deemed to have agreed with the other, whether or not he knows the other's identity.

(3) A conspiracy shall be deemed to continue until its objectives are accomplished, frustrated, or abandoned. "Objectives" include escape from the scene of the crime, distribution of booty, and measures, other than silence, for concealing the crime or obstructing justice in relation to it. A conspiracy shall be deemed abandoned if no overt act to effect its objectives has been committed by any conspirator during the applicable period of limitations.

(4)   It is no defense to a prosecution under this section that the person with whom such person is alleged to have conspired has been acquitted, has not been prosecuted or convicted, has been convicted of a different offense, is immune from prosecution, or is otherwise not subject to justice.

(5)   Conspiracy is an offense of the same class as the crime that was the objective of the conspiracy.

History

Source: L. 1985: Entire article added, p. 2077, § 1, effective March 1, YR-27.

Nita Revised Statutes Title 18 Criminal Code Chapter 18-12-893.13—

Drug Abuse, Prevention, and Control

18-12-893.13 Prohibited acts; penalties.

(1)   (a)   Except as authorized by this chapter and chapter 499, it is unlawful for any person to sell, manufacture, or deliver, or possess with intent to sell, manufacture, or deliver, a controlled substance.

Any person who violates this provision with respect to

(i)   A controlled substance named or described under the U.S. Code of Federal Regulations Title 21, Volume 9, Parts 1300 to end including Opium and opiate, including any salt, compound, derivative, or preparation of opium; Coca leaves and any salt, compound, derivative, or preparation of coca leaves (including cocaine and ecogonine); Opiates; Stimulants; Depressants; and Hallucinogenic substances commits a felony of the second degree.

(b)   Except as provided in this chapter, it is unlawful to sell or deliver in excess of 10 grams of any substance named or described in §1, or any combination thereof, or any mixture containing any such substance. Any person who violates this paragraph commits a felony of the first degree, punishable as provided.

* * *

(f)   Except as authorized by this chapter, it is unlawful for any person to sell, manufacture, or deliver, or possess with intent to sell, manufacture, or deliver, a controlled substance in, on, or within 1,000 feet of the real property comprising a public housing facility at any time. For purposes of this section, the term "real property comprising a public housing facility" means real property, as defined as a public corporation created as a housing authority pursuant to Part I of Chapter 421.

Any person who violates this paragraph with respect to

(i)   A controlled substance named or described in above, commits a felony of the first degree, punishable as provided.

* * *

(iii)   Any other controlled substance, except as lawfully sold, manufactured, or delivered, must be sentenced to pay a $500 fine and to serve 100 hours of public service in addition to any other penalty prescribed by law.

Nita City Ordinances Chapter 157—Graffiti

[HISTORY: Adopted by the City Council of Nita City 9-11-YR-29 as Ord. No. 11-YR-29. Amendments noted where applicable.]

§ 157-2. Definitions.

As used in this chapter, the following terms shall have the meanings indicated:

DEFACE   To cover, mark, write on, paint, color, or otherwise mar, disfigure, or draw on any private or public property of any nature without the express consent of the owner.

GRAFFITI   Any form of inscription, word, figure, marking, or design that is marked, etched, scratched, drawn, or painted on any building, structure, fixture, or other improvement, whether permanent or temporary, including, by way of example only and without limitation, fencing surrounding construction sites, whether public or private, without the consent of the owner of the property, or the owner's authorized agent, that is visible from the private right-of-way.

PUBLIC PLACE   Any place to which the public has access, including but not limited to a public street, road, thoroughfare, sidewalk, bridge, alley, plaza, park, recreation or shopping area, public transportation facility, vehicle used for public transportation, parking lot, or any other parking area, public building, structure, or any municipal parking signs, etc., or area.

§ 157-3. Prohibited acts.

The following acts are prohibited.

(A)   No person shall willfully or maliciously damage, deface, or vandalize any public or private property by painting, writing, drawing, or otherwise inscribing in any fashion graffiti thereon without the express permission or consent of the owner. However, this prohibition shall not apply to easily removable (which are water soluble) chalk markings on public sidewalks or streets, written or drawn in connection with traditional children's games, or in any lawful business or public purpose or activity.

§ 157-6. Violations and penalties.

(A)   Adults who are not parents of offenders as defined in § 157-2 of this chapter. Any adult who violates any of the provisions of this chapter shall, upon conviction thereof, be punished by one or more of the following penalties:

　　(1)   A fine of not less than $500 and not exceeding $1,000.

　　(2)   Imprisonment not to exceed 90 days.

　　(3)   A period of community service not to exceed 90 days.

(B)   Juveniles and/or parent violators as defined in § 157-4 of this chapter.

　　(1)   After the receipt of a warning notice pursuant to § 157-5 (C) of a first violation by a juvenile, when a second graffiti violation is adjudged against the same minor, the parents of the minor shall be subject to prosecution under this section. Violators of this chapter shall be required to perform community service of a period not to exceed 90 days and may be subject to a fine of not less than $500 but no more than $1,000. Additionally, any parent having the care or custody of a minor found to be in violation of this section, if it is adjudged that both the juvenile and the juvenile's parents violated this Graffiti Chapter, they shall be required to perform community service together.

42 U.S.C. § 1437d (1994); Anti-Drug Abuse Act of 1988,

Pub. L. No. 100-690, 102 Stat. 4181 (1988)

§ 1437d(*l*) Leases; terms and conditions; maintenance; termination

Each public housing agency shall utilize leases which—

* * *

(6)   provide that any criminal activity that threatens the health, safety, or right to peaceful enjoyment of the premises by other tenants or any drug-related criminal activity on or off such premises, engaged in by a public housing tenant, any member of the tenant's household, or any guest or other person under the tenant's control, shall be cause for termination of tenancy. . . .

Proposed Jury Instructions

1.   The Court will now instruct you on the law governing this case. You must arrive at your verdict by unanimous vote, applying the law as you are now instructed to the facts as you find them to be.

2.   The plaintiff, the Nita City Housing Authority, seeks to evict Ladonna Johnson and her family from Nita Gardens Public Housing based on a claim that Ms. Johnson breached her lease through the criminal acts of her grandson, Elroy, when he was charged with possession with the intent to sell narcotics, was involved a criminal street gang, and threatened the health, safety, or right to peaceful enjoyment of the premises by other tenants.

The defendant, Ladonna Johnson, denies that her grandson was involved in any criminal activity and affirms that he is not a member of a criminal street gang. She claims her eviction is based on her activities in forming a Tenant Action Committee and that such eviction is prohibited by the terms of her lease and the U.S. Constitution. She further claims that the illegal action of Nita Gardens is prohibited and, therefore, she should not be evicted.

3.   Nita Gardens receives funds from the U.S. government. It is subject to 42 U.S.C. § 1437d (1994), the Anti-Drug Abuse Act of 1988. Section 1437d(l) (6) of that law states:

> Each public housing agency shall utilize leases which . . . (6) provide that any criminal activity that threatens the health, safety, or right to peaceful enjoyment of the premises by other tenants or any drug-related criminal activity on or off such premises, engaged in by a public housing tenant, any member of the tenant's household, or any guest or other person under the tenant's control, shall be cause for termination of tenancy. . . .

4.   The Nita Public Housing Authority lease for Nita Gardens provides in Paragraph 8 Resident Obligations section (C) of the lease

> (C)   Refrain from engaging in, and cause members of Resident's household, any guest, or any other person under Resident's control to refrain from engaging in, any criminal or illegal activity including
>
> (1)   Any criminal, illegal, or other activity that threatens the health, safety, or right to peaceful enjoyment of public housing premises by another resident or a NCHA employee, or that threatens the health or safety of any person residing in the immediate vicinity of the public housing premises;
>
> (2)   Any violent or drug-related criminal activity on or off NCHA property, or any activity resulting in a felony conviction.

5.   In order to evict a tenant the plaintiff has the burden of proving the following propositions:

> (a)   That the defendant, Ladonna Johnson, is a tenant and resident of Nita Gardens;
>
> (b)   Plaintiff, Nita Gardens, is a participant in the Federal Government Housing Program commonly know as the Section 8 New Construction Program and receives rental subsidies from the United States Department of Housing and Urban Development and must comply with 42 U.S.C. § 1437d (1994), The Anti-Drug Abuse Act of 1988.

(c) Plaintiff, Nita Gardens, provided appropriate notice of the breach and eviction to the defendant, Ladonna Johnson.

(d) Defendant, Ladonna Johnson, a member of her family, a guest, or someone under her control engaged in either a criminal activity that threatened the health, safety, or right to peaceful enjoyment of a resident or staff member of Nita Gardens or participated in a violent or drug-related activity on or off Nita Gardens property.

(e) That the defendant, Ladonna Johnson, breached her lease with Nita Gardens, specifically Paragraph 8 Resident Obligations section (C) (1) and (2), by failing to control members of her family from engaging in criminal, illegal, or other activity that threatened the health, safety, or right to peaceful enjoyment of public housing premises or participating in any violent or drug-related activity on or off NCHA property.

If the above propositions are proven, the defendant is in violation of the lease and eviction is appropriate.

6. **Factual issues for the jury.** The factual issues for you to determine are as follows:

(a) Ladonna Johnson is a resident of Nita Gardens;

(b) A lease exists between Nita Gardens and Ladonna Johnson;

(c) Ladonna Johnson breached the Nita Gardens lease by permitting her grandson Elroy to either (1) engage in criminal activity that threatened the health, safety, or right to peaceful enjoyment of the premises at Nita Gardens by a resident or staff member of Nita Gardens; or (2) participated in a violent or drug-related activity on or off the grounds of Nita Gardens.

7. **Defendant's affirmative defense.** The defendant contends the plaintiff has wrongly accused her and her grandson, Elroy Johnson, of breaching the lease and is wrongfully using these clauses to evict her. She further contends her eviction is a direct result of her activity in forming a Tenant Action Committee. Defendant asserts her rights to free speech under the United States Constitution and under Paragraph 7 (B) of the lease, which prohibits retaliation based upon forming or joining a Tenant Action Committee.

8. **Reprisal for tenant's union activity.** The defendant contends that plaintiff has taken this action against the tenant for the tenant's act of joining a tenant's union. The defendant further asserts the plaintiff has taken this action within six months of participation in a tenant's union activity and that the action is a reprisal for the tenant's union activity.

9. **Rebuttable presumption.** The defendant's participation in a tenant's union within six months of the commencement of this action creates a rebuttable presumption that the action is a reprisal against the tenant. It is the responsibility of the plaintiff to rebut this presumption by clear and convincing evidence that such action was not a reprisal against the tenant and that the Plaintiff had sufficient independent justification for taking such action, and would have in fact taken such action, in the same manner and at the same time the action was taken, even if the tenant had not engaged in such activity.

10. If you find from all of the evidence that plaintiff has proven each of the elements necessary to establish grounds for eviction and rebutted the presumption that the action was in reprisal of tenant union activities and that the Defendant has failed to prove either there was no breach of Paragraph 8 of the lease or the Plaintiff has begun this proceeding in retaliation for joining a Tenant Action Committee, then your verdict shall be for the plaintiff. If, on the other hand, you find that any element of the plaintiff's claim has not been established or that the plaintiff retaliated against the defendant's joining a Tenant Action Committee, then your verdict shall be for the defendant.